THE UNPUBLISHED POET

Marjorie Skelly writes of "penciled-in places" and "do not enter" signs. Of silences that "we want more than blood" and others that are "sharper than a new knife." She writes of journeys across the nation and throughout the seasons, sometimes ending in death, sometimes in love. Vulnerable and tough, this poet grapples with the dances and the stillnesses of life.—Patrick T. Reardon, poet, essayist, journalist, and author of five books

Marjorie Skelly's book reminds us of why we read poetry: to find a clarifying vision of what it means to be alive. Whether her poems take us inside a jumbo jet cabin, the big sky country of Montana, a mother's hospital room, or a French countryside, we delight in the journey, one that touches our soul as well as our mind.—Judith Valente, correspondent for PBS-TV and WGLT Radio; author of *The Art of Pausing* and *Atchison Blue*

Marjorie Skelly's writing uses language that soars.—Dennis Held, author of two poetry collections: *Betting on the Night* and *Ourself*

The unpublished poet lives ever in our sister and brother published poets. All of us writers must realize we are apprentices if we are to sustain our essential spiritual growth. Marjorie Skelly's collection of essays, stories, and poems testifies that we are most alive when our pen moves forward, leaving shadow tracks on light paper.—Norbert Krapf, former Indiana Poet Laureate, author of *Catholic Boy Blues*

THE UNPUBLISHED POET

On Not Giving Up on Your Dream

MARJORIE L. SKELLY

THE UNPUBLISHED POET
On Not Giving Up on Your Dream
Marjorie L. Skelly

Edited by Gregory F.A. Pierce
Design and typesetting by Patricia A. Lynch
Cover image © Stanislav Popov under license from Bigstock

Publishing credits for previously published material is on pages 143-144.

Published by In Extenso Press
Distributed exclusively by ACTA Publications, 4848 N. Clark Street,
Chicago, IL 60640, (800) 397-2282, www.actapublications.com

Library of Congress Number: 2015958042
ISBN: 978-087946-987-0
Printed in the United States by Total Printing Systems
Year: 25 24 23 22 21 20 19 18 17 16 15
Printing: 10 9 8 7 6 5 4 3 2 First

✪ Text printed on 30% post-consumer recycled paper

Contents

Dedication

For my husband, Jim Szmurlo,
my daughter, Margaret Fay,
my sister, Carol Gloor

In loving memory of my parents,
Leona and Edward Skelly

Introduction

The Unpublished Poet…well, I guess the title of this book has my name written all over it. Those three words, "the unpublished poet," make me feel as if I am the voice of every writer—even the ones who eventually get published, and even the ones who eventually get frequently published.

Most of us writers spend exponentially more time writing than we do holding published copies of our books in our trembling hands. So the unpublished poet is alive and well in me, even when I see my name in print.

No doubt, it is great to get published; it is the frosting on the cake, the best wine bought from the winery, the first unblemished day of summer spent at the beach. As I write this, I am hoping to recapture my adolescence as I plan to jump up and down, scream with delight, feel the tears of relief run down my face, and have a big party when this book comes in from the printer.

I have identified with unpublished poets, more than with unpublished prose writers, since a poetry book I wrote several years ago made it to finalist status twice with the same university press before being rejected. Still, I have been driven to grief and despair over my short story "Standing in the Dark with my Family" (I am happy to report that this story is included in this book) that three times made it to finalist status, again with a single publisher (this time the prestigious *Glimmer Train Journal*), one time making it near the top of over 1,000 entries. I mention this because many of us unpublished authors know all too well what it is like to get so close to the words "successful author" that we feel as if we are one-thousandth of an inch away, especially when we have developed the habit of entering one contest after another, as I have. We keep giving ourselves the same ridiculous pep talk titled "Well, Maybe This Time." Then, we part with postage and contest entry fees yet one more time, to no avail.

I have been for a while discovering, even before this first book of mine comes out, that getting published takes me out of familiar territory and, strange as it may sound, the familiar can turn into a longstanding friend over the course of a seemingly interminable unpublished life, enough so that it is both difficult and wise to let go of the unpublished saga. Getting published is almost like meeting a new friend who has been born inside of me, but I am not sure that the friendship is going to last.

So, what are we to make of these two worlds, "published" and "un-published," and the rickety bridge that almost never takes us from one side of the chasm to the next? I certainly don't have any answers I trust yet, but I do trust my ongoing desire to continue to write. I would like to think I would have continued to write had I never gotten published at all, but I know that sounds as though it is coming from a person who just took up permanent residence in La La Land. How pure can any of us really be in our "unconditional love" of writing—or singing, or painting, or a host of other art forms for that matter—when we never get the much-needed affirmation from others? Even I know, professional singer that I am not, that singing in the shower is nowhere near as fulfilling as singing in a good choir.

The subtitle of this book, "On Not Giving Up on Your Dream," is so full of an American brand of optimism and the ubiquitous advice to never give up, come hell or high water, that it may make some artists gag. I seriously doubt, however, that there is a poet alive who never considered abandoning both the writing and the attempts to publish. But if you know this rare person, by all means, introduce us. I am pretty sure that most of us poets feel it is better to persevere than not. Maybe that is what makes us poets. The fact that this first book of mine is being published when I am sixty-four years old should be enough encouragement for anyone to keep writing until they pry your cold, dead fingers from your quill pen.

Marjorie L. Skelly
Chicago, Illinois
Thanksgiving Day, 2015

Part One: Essays

Part One consists, in part, of essays reflecting the difficulties and joys of writing and trying to get published. I start with an essay titled "The Importance of Writing, Not Necessarily Publishing, Poetry." This addressed to all unpublished poets, but please don't stop reading if you do not write verse. You still may see a bit of yourself anyway, as most of us have had dreams that do not reach fruition and some of us have dreams that have been thwarted so badly we might refuse to go at them at all ever again. I start the essay with a short quote from the poet Rainer Maria Rilke. As Rilke advises an aspiring young poet (and therefore us as well), the most important thing in life is finding a way to inhabit the unanswerable questions life routinely presents us. He mentions love and how it is stored up for the young poet as though it were an "inheritance."

Note that Rilke's letter is completely absent of writing advice. He knew better. Right now I quiver at the thought that anybody reading this book is seeking advice. The only advice I would dare give a writer is the same advice I would give myself: Trust your own voice more than any other, and find a way to write what only you could have written. A reader should be able to pick up your poem, story, essay, or book and know you "personally" within a matter of minutes. As to what you write about, if you feel something is grabbing you, embrace it as fully as you can. If you are afraid of the subject matter, stay afraid. Fear, as hard as it is to cope with, also provides a boldness that might not be present if you do not write fearlessly.

As crazy as it sounds, the only other thing I have discovered for sure about writing is that some other entity besides myself lives inside me when I write. I know I am never one hundred percent alone when I write. Once while I was night dreaming (I write very late at night much more often than very early in the morning), I found myself in the zone every true writer experiences: sitting in front of the computer and having a thought I had not planned on and did not know whence it came. It was a loud and clear message that needed no deciphering. Whatever, whoever, "spoke" to me informed me that if I did not write I was turning my back on God. That was it; no more words were needed.

I cannot rationally, or even spiritually, explain this; nor would I want to.

One day, I screwed up my courage and told a man I trust about this message. Not only did he not do what I feared most, that is, laugh at me, but the gleam in his eye and the smile on his face needed no translation. I don't often think about this clear-cut message, but I will also never forget it.

In the second essay, which deals with perseverance, giving in, and giving up, I attempt to provide some sort of road map, through my own personal experiences, of the notion that perseverance is not the only show in town. True, I have valued perseverance for more days of my life than not, but I have also discovered its limitations. Perseverance, giving in, and giving up all relate to how we respond to the dreams in our lives. I would not call this second essay "how-to" material, but I believe it illustrates ways of making our dreams come true other than relying on mere perseverance. For me, perseverance has almost always been my default option. But using some discretion and being a bit picky about what we put in to the "perseverance pot" do make a difference in getting results.

In the third essay, I hope I shed new light on what almost all of us have heard in the darkest hours of our lives: "Toughen up!" I invite you to entertain the notion that eating apple pie can be just as beneficial to the artistic temperament as acquiring a tough skin. This essay segues well into the next one, which deals with success and failure and the bill of goods we have been sold when we believe that never the twain shall meet.

Writing the second-to-the-last essay, "Listening to Mozart," put me in touch with the loud voice of grief when it first arrives and then to the way it respectfully is there for us, in this case through Mozart's *Requiem*.

In the last essay of Part One, I shift from writing to singing, as singing has been another lasting love of my life. If you sing in the shower or to put your children to sleep; if you love Bach, Handel, Beethoven, and Mendelssohn; if you have always wanted to sing in a choir or already have done so; then this essay may prove to be as valuable in helping you hold on to your dreams as the ones on poetry.

This ends my introduction to Part One. I will catch up with you again at the beginning of Parts Two and Three. There I hope to engage you in my short stories (Part Two) and my poetry (Part Three). Through storytelling and poetry, I hope that my soul will mirror at least part of yours.

The Importance of Writing,
Not Necessarily Publishing, Poetry

The writer Rainer Maria Rilke wrote to a young poet: "Believe in a love that is being stored up for you like an inheritance, and have faith that in this love there is strength and a blessing so large you can travel as far as you wish without having to step outside of it." He also wrote: "Have patience with everything that remains unsolved in your heart…live in the question."

Rilke did not say anything about us unpublished poets in these two quotes, did he? He knew it is far more important to write than to get published. Good poetry may be either unpublished or published, but unless it is published, insecure monkeys can jump around inside our heads and our bodies can shake from lack of food for the ego. I, for one, would like to proclaim the following directive for my ego: You are the fly that buzzes incessantly around my head; I hereby give you your walking papers.

I imagine at times what wonder and joy there would be for poets if publishing did not exist at all. Oh, sure, publishing is a highly-approved-of task master that is at least some of the time the impetus for getting good things done in the world, like actually communicating with one another. Still, I wonder if we poets could live without ever publishing a word and how the need to be published ever wound up in our DNA in the first place.

But let's go back to Rilke's truly—all sarcasm and cynicism be banished—good advice to the young poet: "Believe in a love that is being stored up for you like an inheritance…." He is right, without doubt. Among other things, we cannot physically touch love; we can't measure love in numbers, even if a high enough number could be found.

"Believe in a *love* that is being stored up for you like an *inheritance*…." I look at the first part of Rilke's quote and part of me wants to stop writing altogether, or at least not engage myself in the sundry soul-killing propositions of trying to get published. What beats having love seen as an inheritance being stored up for you? Getting published? I don't think so.

In the now middle of the second decade of the twenty-first century, there are more writers writing never-to-be-seen manuscripts than books with actual covers on them. Then again, perhaps it has always been this way, but that is another story. But what are we writers to do? Are we to quit trying to get a publisher to publish our work? Are we to publish it ourselves? Do we publish it on the Internet and give it away? If a tree falls in the desert and no one is there…?

I only pose these answerless questions because I can hear tens of thousands of bleary-eyed writers asking them at 2:00 a.m. each morning. I have been one of them most of my life. Why do we continue with the seemingly fruitless journey of trying to get published?

I may be a little out of line addressing this essay to unpublished poets, as I am a poet who has won awards and been published in small literary magazines, but most people have never heard of them, including other poets. I know I have some talent because in the absence of some talent I would not have twice been a finalist for a poetry book contest sponsored by a college press. I could name the press, but guess what? You probably have not heard of it.

With the high level of frustration I have been feeling, I kept trying because I knew my writing is of publishable quality. Furthermore, I have felt I had too much invested in my writing to give up, surrender my will, or engage in the ever popular "letting go." So I was stuck, and the upshot is that sometimes I tried a lot, sometimes a little, sometimes not at all, to get published. A complex dilemma that resulted in a complex response on my part to cope, survive, and sometimes even thrive.

So, why did I continue my mainly unsuccessful attempts to get published? Why did I ignore the stress, the demands, and the inevitable pain that presented themselves at any given moment? Sometimes I was hard on myself. Sometimes I was easy. Most days I was somewhere in the middle. There was no obvious answer as to why I kept trying, and there never will be.

Some days I listened to the cheerleader in me and to others who urged me to forge ahead. Other times the only answer was a glass of wine in front of the television, or better still, a long swim, a bike ride, or attending a choral rehearsal. Still, I would be singing Verdi's *Requiem* and start thinking I should be sending out my poetry book yet again.

I hope I am on to something with the second Rilke quote at the beginning of this essay: "Have patience with everything unsolved in your heart…live in the question." Can you imagine most psychiatrists giving that kind of advice to their clients? That's why I gave up on them years ago.

Yet, Rilke is right, if a right answer is to be had at all. I'm sure that Rilke's advice to the young poet did not deal with the question of how the hell one goes about getting published. That said, I find a strangely reliable comfort in Rilke's words, which is why I know I will return to them in the worst moments of receiving one rejection after another—almost all of them from publishers whose names I am not likely to remember in the same way that they won't remember mine. For me at least, Rilke's profound notion of "living in the question" comes as close to the best answer as to why I write that I have found to date. All other "answers" pale in comparison.

The publisher who thought enough of my poetry book to twice give it finalist status once sent me an email in which she told me that she "did not worry about me because I had both talent AND a dogged type of determination." I capitalized the word "and" because having both talent AND sometimes excessive determination is enough to make me scream in the dark when no one is home.

I wondered where my soul might hide after reading that publisher's comments. I wanted to hide from the terrible knowledge that there are plenty of writers out there who have talent and noses that have been put to the grindstone so often that now they are noseless. I do worry about them; I do worry about me. I know those other "writer souls" are out there. I feel them in my heart's yearnings more than I see them in my mind's eye. I hear the loud silence of all of us knowing, but not saying, that even the marriage of talent to dogged determination may still not produce the coveted offspring of publication. We simply can't even think it most of the time, much less articulate it. The American Dream of being published has lived too long and too unquestioned in our private dreams.

I finally found a publisher who believed in me enough to help me edit and publish this book. But I am no better a poet now than I was before. No, we writers should not give up on our dream of getting published, but we also have to remember that the importance of what we do is the writing itself, for there's "strength and a blessing so large you can travel as far as you wish without having to step outside of it."

Persevere, Give In, or Give Up?

I wish I could ask the genie in the bottle to give me the magic answer regarding the relative value of perseverance, giving in, and giving up on my dreams. Which one should I pick on any given day, and why am I picking it? Still, trial and error—and living long enough—have provided me with three solutions that I can at least live with.

I. Perseverance

In his wonderful poem of only fifty words, *Harlem*, Langston Hughes asks what happens to a dream that is "deferred" too long? Does it "dry up," "fester," "stink," "crust over," "sag"…or "just explode"?

Hughes raises the universal condition of the human heart—having a dream for so long that the dream is "deferred" indefinitely, and then indefinitely, and then…forever. Every poet knows this experience; it is what we do with it that matters.

If the dream of being published means enough to us, many of us lose sleep, obsess over the dream every spare waking moment, and—worst of all—sometimes drive those we love the most away from us. When we are honest with ourselves, we admit that we love this particular dream just as much as we love our spouse, children, and best friends. Heaven forbid that we love this dream even more than the most important people in our lives.

When I have recognized that making my dream of being published come true was causing a nightmare in my relationships with others, I always stepped back for a while to get some sense of perspective.

The imagery in Langston Hughes' poem, in particular, has resonated with me over the years, because I too am a poet. Hughes' dream for Harlem, like mine for publishing, dries, festers, stinks, crusts over, sags, and finally explodes. The word "explodes" really catches my attention because an explosion seems like a fitting thing to happen in the ongoing absence of gratification. For me, I start to explode, just like my dream. I swear and scream too much; the computer screen becomes my worst enemy; and I just wait for a monster with long hairy arms to crash through the screen, grab me by the neck, shake me, and shout "Give up!" That is when I know it is all over, and my soul is in danger of not being able to sustain my dream of publication.

That said, I have come to realize two things. First, if I cannot live without writing poetry and, for that matter, other genres as well, then I have to admit that writing is an integral part of who I am. Another writer I know, Patrick Reardon, told a group attending an event hosting writers at St. Gertrude Catholic Church in Chicago that for him writing is "oxygen." I laughed when I heard that and felt a little bit less lonely as a writer.

Second, although getting published matters, it is not all that I am. I rather look at the process of submitting my work and my other attempts at publication as something akin to climbing Mount Everest: I have to move very slowly most of the time; I have to look forwards and backwards; I have to watch my step at all times; and I know there will be bad weather along the way. And I may not make it to the top.

Getting published feels as difficult as getting to the top of a mountain. Although the terrain may be dangerous and unpredictable, I know I will regret not making the climb. But, as all good mountain climbers must know, lots of rest, breaks, and food help enable the ascent.

II. Giving In

Giving in for me resides somewhere between perseverance and giving up. It does not connote weakness or compromising my dreams. I also don't see giving in as selling out or being wishy-washy.

For example, another dream of mine has been singing in choral groups. It actually comes close to tying for first place with writing. Singing gets me out of the solo experience of writing and into the community of singers. In some ways, I have been more successful as a singer than a writer, because singing with 40-160 other singers can bring me 40-160 times the satisfaction of artistic expression, satisfaction that is immediate and communal.

I use the terminology of "giving in" because for a long time some dictator voice inside me told me I had to choose either writing or singing and that I was a fool for trying to do both and could not possibly honor either art form with my dual attempts. I finally realized that if I did the right balancing act between the two, I could do two things in life I love and neither would be at the expense of the other. Better still, I sometimes sensed that singing brought certain gifts out in me as a writer, and that if I had not sung in a choral group, I never would have written some of my best poems.

When I gave in to singing, I also agonized less over which I was going to do better—writing or singing. I became a more welcoming, less rigid, more sane version of myself and learned that writing and singing feel like two sides of the same passion in me. Although I sense that I am a better writer than a singer, this has never proved to be a very good excuse for me to refrain from singing.

I recently watched a French film titled *The Chorus*, which depicts a teacher who lands a job with orphans and delinquent boys. Naturally, because of the way they are growing up, lacking the support and presence of a parent, these boys are sometimes mean-spirited, full of pranks, and by turns vulnerable, vicious, and open to a better life. Their lives come to fruition only when the teacher forms a chorus and everybody either sings or does something else to contribute to the music making.

The teacher even gives one pre-adolescent boy the job of "being a human music stand." This was the teacher's polite way of telling the boy he was close to tone deaf. At first I thought the teacher was maybe pulling this kid's leg and that it would be humiliating for him to literally "be" the music stand. But sure enough, lovely music is made, the boy holds the scores up for the conductor/ teacher to see, and pride and purpose exude from his young face, even in the absence of a functional singing voice.

Majorie L. Skelly 23

At the end of the day, I have sensed that writing and singing chose me. By "choosing" me, I don't mean "Oh, yes, I am so special, so why would I not be chosen?" Instead, both writing and singing tugged at my soul, although "tug" is too strong of a word for my doing two things that I love. I just mean that by writing and singing—with or without accolades, prestige, fame...or a paycheck—I can live inside my dreams and be fulfilled.

So, I gave in to singing, which resulted in the slow growth of compassion for myself and all others who delve deeply into their dreams, even though we all at times feel at sea, alone in the dark and the tempest, without an anchor.

III. Giving Up

Giving up seems to me both the hardest and easiest thing to do. It is hard because it sometimes feels like defeat, easy because I finally know what the score is. I can let ambition take leave of me for good and not confuse it with giving in to sloth. No more tasks, striving, putting in the hours. This is a form of death, of course, but death, while excruciating, is also the ultimate liberation.

Perhaps the dying would prove to be a bit less excruciating once I knew I was handing over a part of myself that I have hung on to for too long, with little or no hope of the dream being anything more than deferred. Perhaps I would be handing only this old worn out part of myself to the grave, with the knowledge that I had done something irrevocable, burned a bridge behind me, and that there would be no resurrection...at least of this particular dream.

Perhaps now is a good time to look at the intersection of dream and nightmare. I am rather new to giving up. (Perhaps that is due to the "fighting Irish" in me.) So of the three—perseverance, giving in, and giving up—the last one seems the least attractive. But I have given up once, and it was the right thing to do.

Feel free to think to yourself, "What does Marjorie know about giving up? She says she's new to giving up, and she just had her first book published." I won't be offended. Let's just walk down this path together then, see what we find when we take Robert Frost's road less traveled. Perhaps that will have made all of the difference—you and me being pioneers in this new territory of giving up. Giving up, really permanently giving up, is so un-American. We have pulled ourselves up by our bootstraps so often, so relentlessly, that it's a wonder we have any boots…or for that matter any self, left at all. A car's tank of gas is good for maybe 250-300 miles, and then when those miles have been driven, we seem stunned that a car is incapable of running on empty. And that is what relentless ambition can do—make you "run" on empty.

For better or for worse, "for good or for ill," this is where we will reside with Langston Hughes: Does our dream explode if we give up? I wonder at the starkness of the words of Hughes' poem. Just what were the life circumstances of this particular poet that made him so very much in tune with the reality of the dying and dead dream? The end of the poem brings with it the probable end of a dream deferred.

I am glad I took a better look at this poem for this essay, because now I realize that my response to giving up is more complex than I thought it would be. I am thinking of my own recent "official" giving up on something that mattered to me when I graduated from college and for many years after that: being a high school English teacher. In 1973, the year I graduated from college, there was no plethora of teaching jobs. I looked for a job for over two years and then finally took one out of state in New York; I was not even certified to teach in New York when I took the job. I was not certified when I quit the job either.

I only lasted at the job for a few months in the midst of unexpected weight loss, severe insomnia, isolation, and classrooms filled with 16-year-old boys and girls, some of them, I felt, just dying to get me any way they could. Being a good disciplinarian, it goes without saying, was not only not my strong suit; it was my downfall. That and getting hired two and a half weeks before the first day of school, knowing two other humans in my new landscape of upstate New York, and leaving every last detail of the familiar life behind me in Chicago. By the time I resigned, I felt as though I was 24 going on 50.

Flash forward to April 2015, in the midst of necessarily having to part with some of the material world due to remodeling our condo, I took my last look at my Illinois State Teaching Certificate, saying I was qualified to teach grades six-twelve. I had not renewed it since 2000. Staring at this certificate felt like falling into a black hole and conjured up a past of incessantly looking for jobs, having hideous substitute teaching experiences, breaking up brawls between adolescent boys, literally being propositioned in the classroom, and having my wallet stolen in that same classroom while I was still in it. I remembered human snot that kids put on my bicycle seat; a teacher being hospitalized after a student took a swing at her in the classroom; the disappearance of children during visits to their lockers, the bathroom, and the counselor's office; and last, but far from least, "Get your white, m-f ass out of this class," uttered by a boy within ten seconds of my entry into the classroom and before I put my name on the blackboard. It goes without saying that my barbed retort fell on deaf ears. So did at least ninety percent of what I tried to teach.

Even the one longer stint I had as a physical education aide at a Chicago suburban school provided me with another journey into chaos and mismanagement. I liked my co-workers well enough, but for the full year I worked part-time there I never was given a key to get back into the building after I did recess duty. How was it that the key I never got, for a full academic year, no less, was frequently given to day-to-day substitute teachers but not to me, a regular employee? No one even bothered to try to give me a believable answer to that question.

Bona fide terror and anger set in the day, all exaggeration aside, when I was left both *alone* and *to my own devices* to literally supervise close to *two hundred* middle-school kids outdoors. The teacher I was working with that day was called back into the building for, presumably, something extremely important, while I was left, through no choice of my own, supervising a clearly illegal number of children by myself. When I urged a student to go inside the building once the bell rang, he refused many times. I put my hand on his shoulder to nudge him, as all nudging with words could not get him to budge an inch. He went off on me telling me that I was "just" an aide and how dare I touch him and he was going to tell his parents about my touching him.

Clint Eastwood intervened for me within seconds when I heard myself state to the student in no uncertain terms, "Go ahead and make my day," followed by a loud, "Do you really think I give a damn about what you will do?" Finally, everybody got back inside the building. For the amount of energy I used within less than an hour, I might have been able to take on Darth Vader or Rocky Balboa.

I was so furious that I screamed at the school secretary while simultaneously telling her that I knew I should not be screaming at her. Fortunately, she was the nice mellow type who had probably seen the likes of me on more than one occasion. Her body language announced to me in no uncertain terms that she both knew I was right and that she also knew that not a damn thing would be done about it.

I finally deleted part of my past in April of 2015. Not only did I trash my teaching certificate, I shredded it. In hindsight, I wish I had burned it. It may have been more gratifying to see my terrible experiences go up in smoke and become ashes. From dust this former dream came, and to dust it returned. I honestly think that if I could have murdered my teaching past, I would have done so. Finally, better late than never, I had given up.

So, I gave up on the dream of being a teacher. I don't feel bad about that. It was not oxygen for me. It was not writing or singing. It was the right decision—for me, not for somebody else. And that is how I know that giving up is just as valid a choice as perseverance or giving in.

Thick Skin Is Highly Overrated

How many times have we unpublished poets heard about the importance of developing a thick skin? Well, personally I have yet to be either inspired by, or convinced of, the value of a deep, dense epidermis.

I, for one, would not mind it at all if no one ever again proclaimed the virtue of having a thick skin, which roundly suggests toughness and is always accompanied by the prescription to get one as quickly as possible. After all, if we are not tough, we may as well have "weak kneed" embroidered on to our pants and the word "sissy" painted on our foreheads. We might even be accused of having thin skin, which I presume belongs to people who are so fragile that if their sparse, faint, feeble, weak body covering were to peel off it would expose nothing but their bleeding heart.

I want to know what happened to the lost art of falling apart. If we fall apart, we can be put back together; whereas if we thrive based on the depth of our skin, do we not set up a barrier that keeps us in a constant state of posing positively for the world? Why shouldn't we let that world know that we care what happens to us, that we are disappointed or sad or depressed or angry or disgusted or even hurt? So what if something gets under our skin? If it does, isn't having a thick skin a detriment, since it makes it all the harder to get the damn thing out?

I have heard of the importance of having thick skin so many times that in my better moments this both well-meant and condescending advice goes in one ear and right out the other (which makes it helpful that no one has advised me to get thicker ear membranes). I suspect that those who cheer the loudest for a thick skin may never have had much need of one themselves. In my worst moments, however, I think the advice must have some merit, but no one has ever told me exactly how to thicken my skin, leaving me thick-skin-impaired, which should qualify me for some sort of federal aid.

Thick is to skin as apple pie is to America. That said, I'd opt for the apple pie any day of the week, thank you. With all of the advice that has been meted out to me as to what the texture of my skin should be, for my part I would rather be sitting with a menu inside a cozy Bakers' Square booth, waiting for Apple Cliché to come out of the oven and melt in my mouth from the outpouring of cream added to the pie. Put the tough skin back where it does its job best: on those whose job requires thick-skinnedness. Politicans, maybe, lawyers, of course, athletes, probably. Parents, don't you know it. But why should artists be thick-skinned, especially the poets? I thought we were all supposed to be quivering nerves of emotion.

❧ ❧

Some of the best poets I can think of have partially, or totally, fallen apart or at least become very affected by people's responses to their poems. The poet Maxine Kumin stayed away from her pen for ten years, give or take a few, after receiving some less-than-palatable feedback on her poems. She later went on to win the Pulitzer Prize for Poetry in 1973.

When I first learned about Kumin spending so many years not writing poetry, the only lens I could see her through was my own experience. I was a gifted writer who lost a decade of her writing life to the more-mean-spirited-than-necessary comments from a writer likely well-versed in the art of soul killing.

Hearing Kumin's story, I remembered some of the more negative things about my experience in the undergraduate writers' workshop in fiction at the University of Iowa in the early 1970s. I got out lucky, in that the worst thing anybody said about my writing was that it suffered from "mental masturbation."

I will never forget the day before class when some joyous slob of a professor (or was he only a teaching assistant?) literally leered over the manuscript of some earnest young writer, announcing to all passersby in the hallway that he was going to "rip this manuscript into smithereens." I was nineteen years old and felt like throwing a pie in his face—apple if necessary. Can't you just feel his good intentions and constructive criticism in your heart, even today?

I keep thinking of Sylvia Plath, who, unlike Maxine Kumin, has a poetic legacy that has extended a bit more into the "mainstream," if you will. Actress Gwyneth Paltrow played her in the movie *Sylvia*, and both Diane Keaton and Woody Allen made a reference to the Plath poetry book *Ariel* in the Woody Allen film *Annie Hall*.

Whether you like Plath's poetry, think she may have dealt with her husband a bit too harshly, judge her for having left two small children behind due to her suicide—it is hard to dispute that among American poets she is considered one of the best.

❧ ❦

But I see that I have digressed. I mention these two poets to point to the vulnerability they experienced in both their life and their writing. I never once thought of either writer as having thick, or for that matter thin, skin. They were who they were, both exceptional writers who, at the end of the day, exhibited strengths that were indubitably more related to the nature of their souls and talents than to the thickness of their skin.

Furthermore, although Plath got much of her work published while she was still alive, it was she who said "Nothing stinks like a pile of unpublished writing." I take both solace and anxiety from that quote. Even someone bearing literary gifts as extraordinary as Sylvia Plath had a visceral need to get her work published.

Yes, there is a unique quality to the stench of the unpublished, the nastiness of its ongoing physical presence haunting the kitchen table or office desk.

The way the pile smirks at you leaves you no choice but to smirk back. It produces anxiety because for reasons you cannot even fully explain to yourself, much less to someone else, the drive to get published gets written all over a poet's soul. And you sometimes notice, like it or not, that yes, your writing is, *in fact*, getting better and that, yes, seeing some of it published might, *in fact*, prove it.

I know many poets roughly at the same place in their writing life that I am. We are not famous. We will probably never be a household name. We might never make any real money from our writing, and most likely we will never make a living from it. Our struggle with those facts, however they manifest themselves, is something none of us enjoys. That said, I remember no conversations I have had with other writers about the benefits of thick skin or the importance of developing some forthwith. Instead, at best, we feel connected and supportive and do not have to explain our plight to one another—as we all share roughly the same one, however different the details of that plight may be.

How many times have I heard of the importance of having thick skin? Enough that I felt the need to write about it. Now it is time to take some solace in the "medium thickness" of my cat's fur. She has waited patiently for my attention the entire time she has sat on my lap as I tried to type and pet her at the same time. She knows nothing at all of the importance of thick skin. She is, after all, a cat and not an armadillo. And when she meows, I stroke her back, and for a few precious moments there is no grindstone I am pressing my face against, just her wet nose against mine.

Success and Failure: Joined at the Hip

They both arrive in our lives, at times in different guise. Tonight, Success will show up with more cleavage while Failure is still trying to find a bra that fits. Though neither knows it, the ego trip for both of them is temporary.

The next day when the sun rises, they will both get confused, since they each thought Time always stood still for them, their egos large enough to block out light, or at least eclipse it for a while. Failure looks pretty today in her humility: a dress that barely, but noticeably, shows off her great legs. Success did not get a good night's sleep, however. Her dreams of herself slipped into nightmares that presented in dark raccoon eyes with yesterday's eyeliner shaping the top of her nose in lieu of her eyes.

That night they will meet in their favorite bar, share a beer, then a cognac, then part their separate ways as if it were only a one-night stand…which it ain't…which it ne'r was…and ne'r will be. Still, it is hard to think of them as co-dependent as they both think they can live without the other.

Failure seems to be the top dog as she routinely refuses to leave, even when asked politely to do so. You would think she would be happy to depart, as she just can't stand the sight of Success. And Success? She's that sweet tooth in your mouth that makes you want to spit out all nutrition and live on chocolate. And the craving never ends. She also suffers from acute amnesia, never realizing that Failure happens to be her mother, no matter how incestuous that may seem after everybody who is anybody saw them both together in that bar.

Failure's a lot stronger than success as she knows labor pains, blood, and birth. She is also as enlightened as a Buddhist in his last life as she realizes that mistakes are just that: mis-hyphen-takes. Since she has no concept of self at all, she doesn't even give a second thought to the pronoun "his" in the previous sentence referring to the "she" that she supposedly is. As for mis-hyphen-takes, Failure knows that the only way to get to the take is to miss it often, often enough that you can finally orbit it and see it at a distance before you can close in upon it. Further, think as well of a basketball player repeatedly missing the hoop until eventually hoop, player, and ball meld into one until the ball going through the net becomes a work of art.

What if Failure were Success and Success Failure? This would end much of a poet's misery. We all think we know Failure as well as the back of our hands, whereas Success is the visible polish of the manicure, often appearing in bright red so as not to be missed. However, Failure, much more pervasive, *is* the back of our hands: the wrinkled, calloused world where hangnails live and warts abound. She covers more territory and is as familiar to us as our own mortality. And yet we call *her* Failure?

Would we artists all be lost if both words were removed from the dictionary? Or perhaps they both might appear in a thesaurus: success: synonym failure; failure: see success.

Too confusing, right? In your heart of hearts, though, haven't you really wanted to off both relentless demons? What a house of cards they are.

Somewhere in a foreign country (its name escapes me) there are no words at all for self-hatred or self-deprecation. Wonder how the citizenry fares?

Epilogue

Please don't ask me if what I just wrote is a success or a failure. All by way of saying thank you for honoring both my ignorance and my intelligence. And don't be fooled either: Ignorance is Success and Intelligence is Failure. And yes, Intelligence *really* is Failure—good God, all that gray matter in our brains. The color gray…is it any wonder that we can't think clearly?

Finally, the same holds true, perhaps even more so, for getting my writing published. Buying a lottery ticket holds more promise of winning big than submitting a manuscript.

So why do I bother with manicures, eyeliner, cognac, with the nightmare of trying to get published? Hell, what do I know? If I knew the answer to that question, I'd be successful.

Part Two: Stories

Stories are like poetry and essays, except when they're not. They are like essays because they are in prose and like poetry because they take poetic license with the facts in order to get at greater truths. All three are supposed to be artfully written.

In "White Stars, Black Night," it is Martin Luther King's birthday. The temperature is sub-zero, so come sit with me in a Chicago bar in the 1990s when smoking and racism were still allowed. Who among us takes an active stance against racism, and who wants to do so but doesn't out of fear, complacency, or the simple, understandable need to get away from it all for one night? We dream of ending injustice for others and ourselves. We take action, remain passive, and escape from the familiar world. We do this in silence and conversation.

Then, sit with me on the Armitage Avenue bus. You are done with a work day along with other riders. When you least expect it, the strangest things can occur. They make you laugh out loud, become stone silent, and fill you with compassion or the indifference of looking away.

Next, it is one of those brutally hot afternoons when swimming is the only cure for sitting down all day at work. Though temporary, the cure works.

When you read "Looking for Home," the Chicago heat is still in full force along with unbearable humidity. Reality, however, is not in control, and home is elusive.

"Standing in the Dark with my Family" is surrealistic in a different way than "Looking for Home." What is more real, the dream or our waking hours? Perhaps we will never know for sure as we continue to walk across the bridge between the two in terror and relief, sorrow and joy, as the river beneath us always flows.

Finally, I end with two non-fiction pieces, one pertaining to grief and the other about singing and singers. Just in case you think my writing (and my life) too dark, these stories show how music lifts me up.

White Stars, Black Night

In the lovely silent part of my relationship with Alex, my mind drifts in and out of the past and present. I look around and notice that all but a few bar stools are occupied by white men wearing drunk, bored, and indifferent faces, sometimes all three. I catch myself; who am I to judge white men in a bar? Maybe they need to escape from reality as much as I do. One of the few women, the most animated of the group, looks hostile one moment and breaks into loud laughter the next as she drinks whiskey and chain smokes cigarettes. Asians, whites, and blacks sit at wooden tables, occasionally all of them appearing at the same table. I think of Martin Luther King, Jr., as I have been doing most of the day. It is his birthday. He was only thirty-nine when he died.

I find myself trying to go back in time to Atlanta, Georgia, in 1929, and imagine what the birth of Martin Luther King looked like. Perhaps his parents were suffering from the Depression as they stared down at their newborn in his crib. They may have imagined something great for this child or just as likely were concerned about all that goes into the daily grind of the often selfless job of raising a child. I sense that neither the terrible economic times nor high-minded dreams for their son mattered as much as holding him in their arms.

"So, how was your day?" I ask Alex, after sipping my rum and coke. My voice sounds so odd and public as it breaks through my meanderings about the past.

"The usual. If the Chicago Board of Education makes one more mistake with my paycheck, I'll scream! Working in a class filled with the behaviorally challenged isn't hard enough. I also have to deal with bureaucrats at Central Office just to get a paycheck. God, Annie, did I tell you about my most recent payroll nightmare? I called Central first and let the phone ring 103 times. Can you believe I actually counted?"

"Yes, I've done that before."

"Then I was put on hold for twenty minutes only to be told that the secretary was on break. I was so pissed off that I drove down to Central to straighten the mess out. There's nothing like a face-to-face confrontation with a bureaucrat who cannot hide behind a ringing phone. If you ask me, these people are on break all day!"

"See why I no longer work for the Chicago Board?"

"Yeah, but now your salary has been cut almost in half," Alex reminds me.

"So has my psychiatry bill."

Alex smiles, and we are back to silence. Now, I wonder if I will ever have children with Alex and if they will grow up suffering from being raised in an interracial family. I recall with striking clarity that in 1969 I worked at Maryhaven, a nursing home in Glenview, a suburb north of Chicago. One of my co-workers, a pale, blonde teenager, once walked down the street with one of the Maryhaven cooks, a black man. She later told me that people were gaping at them—revealing, not hiding, their surprise that pale and black went side by side.

I contemplate how long it has taken most of us to advance from gaping to anything approximating color blindness. And how very strange, I think, that I call myself white when my skin is not the color of chalk, and Alex calls himself black when in truth, he is dark brown. I have an epiphany of sorts when I realize that white people are far less accurate about calling themselves white than black people are about naming the color of their skin; some people really do have black skin. My mind spins, and I don't know where it is going the moment I wonder how we white people began to call ourselves "white" in the first place. Was it an awful sub-conscious thing at work; were we so afraid of being black that we resorted to the total absence of color at all? The insidious depth of racism chills me at that very moment, and I begin looking at the skin on both of my arms as if I were seeing it for the first time.

"Annie, you okay?"

I ask myself how much has really changed since 1968, when James Earl Ray assassinated Dr. King, before I respond to Alex. I have no answer as I keep looking at my skin, as if I am putting it under a microscope for scientific observation.

"Oh, I am just lost in reverie," I say lamely as I reach for alcohol. Alex's questioning eyes tell me he does not buy this, but he drops the inquiry.

Remembering important historical dates is not enough. I should be doing something in the world to bring about racial equality. I would not be worrying about the future so much in my own quiet, private world if there still was not so much racial disparity in the loud, public world. How could I possibly be paying King his due by sitting in a cozy Chicago bar with Alex, never mind how exhausted both of us are from the grind of our teaching jobs? Tired of my own mental ramblings, I ask Alex where he was on the day of King's assassination.

"Is that question of the same ilk as where were you on the day that Kennedy was assassinated?"

"I suppose so. But, hey, I'm giving you a break on your test of total recall, since 1968 is more recent than 1963 and we are both middle-aged and suffering from a little memory loss."

"Hey, babe, don't give me any of that middle-age memory loss stuff. I'm 39, and you're 41!"

"Yeah, yeah," I say, unable to hide my smile. Anyway, where were you, Mr. Memory?"

"You know I just can't remember. No, seriously now, I was a sophomore in high school in Memphis, Tennessee."

"I didn't know you lived in Memphis."

"I did. Anyway, I was at home really sick in bed with a very high fever, watching television but wanting to read, but I was too sick for that. My mother offered me freshly squeezed orange juice, her antidote for illness. I was watching Leave it to Beaver, and I remember that day as if it were yesterday. I craved a piece of cake that my mother offered me, but my throat hurt so badly that I couldn't eat it."

"C'mon now, Alex. You're telling me that you can remember craving cake on one particular day twenty-five years ago!"

"I can because my mom's cake was always so delicious, so smooth, and just the right texture. She used to make it for me regularly and had baked one that very day. I wanted that cake so badly, but my throat just would not tolerate anything but juice."

"I apologize. Go on."

"Well, *Beaver* was interrupted by a news bulletin. I knew deep inside me that something bad was coming since I had those same horrible jitters I had at track meets the moment my feet flew from the starting line. I remember Walter Cronkite, his voice so somber."

Now, I recall Cronkite, but on the day of President Kennedy's assassination, how he had looked when he removed his glasses, the one small tear in the corner of his eye.

"I remember Cronkite, that the moment I saw him I didn't want to see him. Within seconds, I knew that King had been shot. My mother tripped over a chair and spilled all of the orange juice on my lap. I remember the sticky, sweet smell. I remember my fever going up. I remember...."

Alex stops talking. The chain-smoking whiskey-drinking woman at the bar now faces him and has been listening to him without his knowing it. I catch her face for a moment as I try to ensure that she does not pick up on my observing her. She has lost the highs and lows of too much booze, replacing them with something like compassion in her eyes. The jukebox is now playing Kansas: "All we are is dust in the wind."

Then, I see tears falling down her face—long fluid streaks turning black from her mascara. She orders another whiskey to deal with her compassion. I see a tear in the corner of Alex's eye and know that he would not choose to let it fall.

New jukebox lyrics distract us with Percy Sledge: "When a man loves a woman...." His great black voice drowns out the bar talk, lingers as effortlessly as the moon slipping behind a cloud in the sky, shining and fading in the great expanse of the cloud.

I respectfully turn my eyes away from Alex as he lowers his into his drink. I look at the wooden bar again; it strikes me as substantial with its smooth mahogany shine. Lemon dust polish mingles with scents of stale beer, second-hand smoke, french fries, and barbecued chicken wings. I know that even though this is the first time I have ever had a drink here I could fall in love with this place—its coziness and cleanliness, even a hint of an older world of charms so absent from other bars and restaurants I frequented in the early 1990's. Even the cigarette smoke in the air was easy to endure in the presence of such fabulous background music.

I order white wine for myself and notice a man at the bar who is drunker than the rest. He shouts at the bartender to get him another Black Russian. When that comes, he notes that the bartender has made him a White Russian.

"Take that silly-ass girl drink and throw it out," he says to the thin Hispanic bartender, who wears his necessary poker face as he correctly makes the man a Black Russian. I watch him down the drink in about twenty seconds flat at which point he again shouts, even louder, "Get it right this time, jackass! Give me a White Russian." The bartender returns to the drunk, the beginning of fear showing in his eyes, and hands him a Black Russian. The drunk takes one look at it and yells, "Don't you listen, you stupid spic! This time I wanted a White Russian." Several White Russians are promptly served up.

Some barflies break out into nervous laughter while others take up floor watching. We table-sitters eventually resume our table talk, secure in our physical distance from the bar.

"Maybe we should go home," I suggest.

"Yeah, I'll finish my drink, and we'll leave."

I listen to the Beatles song, "Yesterday," about being half the man I used to be and Alex resumes his recollections. "When King died, a part of me died. I almost did die, for real. My fever shot up to 106 degrees, and I went to the hospital. So, where were you on that day?"

I hold Alex's hand tightly in mine. "I was a junior in high school." As I start to speak, I notice that the man drinking the White Russians is getting louder and sicker looking. "I was watching television too," I continue with one eye on the drunk. "I knew Chicago would be up for grabs now. On a personal level, I had been thinking about suicide long before King's death."

"You never told me that you were suicidal!" Alex cannot hide the alarm and love on his face. "Why did you want to kill yourself?"

"I had acne, an inferiority complex, an indifferent father, a depressed mother, hideous menstrual cramps...."

"A case of teenageritis?"

"Yeah. I also hated my ugly hair and warts."

"Full of self-love, huh?"

I nod. "I won't continue with the litany of my adolescent angst. Anyway, when I heard the news, I was mad. I was furious. It made me want to live...."

Stop it, stop it, stop it! You are too loud, too sincere, too....

Now, the drunk is standing near enough to hear me. He must have crept toward me at the height of my desire to live. He eyes Alex and me as though we are a couple who would do well to live on Pluto.

"Hey, bith," he says, but I know he means bitch. "Hey," he shouts, nearly falling on top of me. "What time is it?"

"Time for you to go home," I say with total sobriety. Why didn't I just give the man clock time?

"Hey, bitch," he says, enunciating "bitch" with enormous effort. "Damn you; that's not what I axed for."

Alex stands up and puts his coat on. "It's almost seven. My God, it's late!"

"Hey, nigger, I'm talking to this girl, not you!"

Alex turns toward the exit sign, takes a few steps in that direction, then hesitates.

"Did I hear you right?" I shout at the man, knowing that I had.

"Ya' betcha did, girlie! In case you didn't, let me riterate it again. I don want no nigger interruptin' my conversation wit you!"

Sweat drips down my armpits as I rise to put on my coat. I imagine the drunk seeing the sweat, delighting in it. I know that I will choke on my own silence, so I raise my arm quickly, almost involuntarily, at the drunk.

"Nobody calls my man a nigger. Nobody. Nobody calls any man a nigger!"

This voice of mine, where was it coming from? I did not premeditate these words; they seemed to rise up from my own sweat.

The drunk sways back and forth for a moment, looking to hold on to something, anything. Then, he cups one hand over his ear and says, "S'cuse me, Missy. I do believe I heard somethin' you could not possibly be sayin'."

"You heard me right!" I shout so loudly that the bartender turns his head and glares at us. A couple of customers look up from their drinks, clearly interested in this diversion from their own conversations.

I make my hand into a tight fist, my fingers digging into my palm. About an inch from the man's nose, I hear one man cry out, "Go get him! He deserves it!" Then, I feel Alex's hand pushing my fist back to a near miss with my chin.

We both throw money on the table and start to run outside, catching a quick glimpse of the man falling to the floor without a single blow delivered. Little pools of saliva congregate on his lips and the corners of his wrinkled chin. I run forward and look backward at the same time, still catching brief visual flashes of the inside of the bar. The bartender has clearly taken center stage and looks understandably annoyed at what our scene might do for business. A few people, scared like us, have left the premises. The woman at the bar looks as though she will help the drunk to his feet but then walks away from him. Mainly the conversations continue and the drinks keep on coming.

Shocked by the cold, we run hand in hand, our grasp certain, ice and snow underneath our feet. I am amazed at how well I can remember the sky that night and startled by how, even now, I can, in the midst of terrible fear, conjure up imagery, knowing the origin of this imagery no better than where my final words to the drunk came from.

Thick black velvet stitched together with needle points of vibrant white stars, an immense black garment sheltering us all. Without this sky, the stars would refuse to shine. Were it not for stars, the sky would live in eternity as only a testament to darkness.

We wait for a bus, any bus. My eyes catch the menace and beauty of the full moon, set like a diamond in the black sky. Alex has retreated into the safety of his head phones. He turns more meaningfully away from me; I note his closed eyes. A seductive woman's voice on the radio whispers to him, "Big boys don't cry. Big boys don't cry." He turns the volume down.

We board a bus that is populated with no one but the two of us and the driver. Alex falls asleep, his head on my shoulder. I sit up straighter and straighter each time the bus comes to a jerking halt, and I refuse to close my eyes.

Bus Fare

Danny sits next to me on the Armitage Avenue bus going east. He looks pale to me, more so than usual. I hope he isn't sick or anything. I think he should be given more breaks at work so that he can go outside and get some fresh air. Well, as fresh as the air can be on any given day in Chicago.

That's why I take him and the other adults out jogging as much as possible. I know that jogging is not the kind of thing I am supposed to be teaching them, but it's a good way to break up the day. Besides, they get flabby sitting around all day. Looking at Danny now, I see he isn't as flabby as he was a year ago, so I guess the exercise is paying off. Since my job title is Training Specialist, I may as well train the adults in whatever specialized way I see fit. The bureaucracy that spits out my paycheck every two weeks says I am supposed to be preparing these people to pass a high school equivalency test. Ridiculous, ill-founded optimism. They can't even spell their names.

"Cardogram, Laurie, that what it was. Doc goofed up on that. Doc don't want that to happen to me. I go to doctor today, Laurie. Check up."

"I hope everything is all right with you, Danny," I say sympathetically, enunciating each word, hoping I don't sound like an elocution teacher.

"Hope so, hope so," he says, tilting his large blond head to one side. "Something 'bout co, co-li-tis. Might have problem there. Might have problem there."

"Well, it is good that you are going to have a check-up then, Danny. That is important."

"Yeah. Goof up on my dad, they did. I tell you. I tell you, goof up. I tell you. Whole, whole family surprised. Dad, sixty-two. Couldn't believe it. Cardi, cardigram wrong."

"Danny, I'm really sorry about your father." I reach out and touch his pink hand; it is covered with horrible smelling incense from the job he does at the sheltered workshop where I teach.

"Thanks, thanks, Laurie."

In my spare time at the workshop, I have often gone into the large, poorly ventilated room to watch Danny do his job. I am always surprised by the starkness of the environment that Danny and the others work in. Walls with no paintings, hard gray floors and table tops—even the poster boards that Danny's friends count and put in boxes are without color.

But Danny is luckier. He counts bright pink incense sticks; slowly he arrives at the number ten and puts these sticks into plastic bags. As I look at him on the bus now, and then at my own two hands, I am amazed to think that I have always known I have ten fingers.

"Danny, are you going on the picnic with us tomorrow?"

"Hope so. Hope so. If checkup okay, I go. I go."

"That's great, Danny. I hope you can come."

"I do. So do I."

"Did you go on the picnic last year, Danny?"

"Think so."

"How was it?"

"Fun times, Laurie, fun times. I won a, I won a, won…."

He stops talking for a moment. I look intently at his eyes, and I see the struggle for words in them. I try to imagine what is going on in his brain at this very moment. Something inside tells me that if I could only listen to the rhythms of his heart, I could finish the sentence within him.

"What did you win, Danny?"

"Fifty cents, Laurie! Fifty cents."

"That's wonderful, Danny!" His grin is bigger than a child's. "I hope you didn't spend it all in one place."

"Spend one place."

"Danny, what *did* you do with your fifty cents?"

"Li-cense I gonna go get, Laurie." He turns around and faces me, and our knees touch. His voice becomes serious and quiet now; he seems earnest about something. "Propose to you, Laurie. Got to go Justice of Peace."

"That's nice, Danny!" As always, I am flattered by Danny's use of the word "propose." Like the other adults I work with, he wants to be certain that he asks an important question the right way.

"Cubs Park honeymoon."

I burst out laughing. I just can't help it. I start to see the two of us in the seventh inning stretch, he in his tux and I in my white, knowing that the Cubs will lose. I'm tempted to tell him that although he's not my type, he's cute.

"What you laughing 'bout?" He doesn't look hurt. I'm relieved.

"You're just so funny, Danny." He starts laughing now, which makes me laugh even harder because I know he doesn't know what he is laughing about.

"What's so funny?" asks Danny, genuine innocence in his voice.

"I, I..." I cannot talk because I'm trying to catch my breath. My stomach hurts, and tears are in my eyes. I start to laugh even harder. I realize it doesn't make any difference to know exactly what we are laughing about.

In their confusion, passengers on the bus stare at us. I sense their suppressed patronizing judgment of us, the questionable benevolence marking their faces as they try to deal with what they sense: "retardation," the word that nobody will say out loud on a bus or even at a sheltered workshop. Why in the hell don't they just laugh with us?

The bus lumbers over a badly pitted section of Armitage until it stops at Halsted. Near the front of the bus, a man stands up. His tattered gray suit is practically falling off him, and there's an empty wine bottle sticking out of his pants pocket. I hear the sound of continuous liquid hitting the floor.

"Missy, look at man. Missy, wet, he's wet. Why wet?"

I cannot answer Danny, and I cannot stand the sound, the soft flow. I cannot look at the wino, and I know he is urinating. He keeps on doing it; he just won't stop.

No one stares at the man. No one stares at Danny. Our eyes are all frozen, looking straight ahead. Our collective silence force us to hear the slow, slow dripping. We are all asking ourselves the same question: When, when will it stop? No one moves.

But the bus driver is on to him. He stops at the corner, puts the bus in park, and heads back to the guy. We know what's coming. I don't want to look. I can hear it. I can hear the fist hitting the wino's face.

"Ouch," Danny says. "Ouch!"

"Get yaw ass off this bus this minute!"

"Swear, Laurie, swear," Danny whispers.

"But who I harm? Who I harm?" asks the man crumpled on the floor. I can see the whole thing out of the corner of my eye.

"Don't ask no questions, you jive-ass bastard!"

"Who I harm, who I harm?" Danny repeats with the man.

"Man, you get off this minute. You don't and I'm gonna kick your butt out."

"Go 'head, go 'head, don't care, don't care."

I place my fingers in my ears, but I still can hear the wino's bones cracking against pavement and see the satisfaction in the body language of the bus driver: arms akimbo and a smirk on his face, telling everyone that he fears no retribution. He is, after all, keeping us safe. The unspoken question "Safe from what?" sits in my mouth like a lump of gristle—hard to chew and swallow, hard to digest.

"Hurt," says Danny. The doors slam shut, then briefly open to release two people and admit two more.

I see a woman sitting across the aisle talking to her friend. Her voice has no humor in it, just defiance. "I tell you, I tell you, I have had it up to here," she says as she points to the place where her neck meets her head.

It is time for Danny and me to get off. As we lumber to the front of the bus, I see the eyes of the other passengers on him again. We climb down the stairs, and Danny turns to the bus driver and says, "God bless you." The driver cannot bear to look at Danny.

When we are on the street, I walk Danny to his front door to make sure his mother sees he got home safely. She smiles at me through the living room window. I'm comforted knowing that she is going with Danny to the doctor's.

Once Danny is inside, I say goodbye, see you tomorrow, and start to walk back to the bus stop to catch my bus home. I'm a block away from Danny's house when I hear him calling after me.

"Wait, Laurie, wait."

I stop walking, and he runs up to me, his shirt falling out of his loose pants. "For you, Laurie. I save it for you! Fifty cents! Fifty cents! Spend one place. Spend one place."

My eyes lock with Danny's as he presses the palm of my right hand open to put two quarters in it. He pushes my fingers over the coins until he is sure they will not slip out of my hand. "Married," he says, with triumph and finality in his voice.

For a minute, I stand, rigid and speechless as a statue, holding the quarters tightly in my hand.

"Yes," I finally say. "Married."

Swimming

The best thing about water was that she never had to fight it. Pool water always held her up and never felt like an obstacle to her. Swimming, strangely, was like a completed sentence for her; it did not have to be proofread like almost 100 percent of all the documents she worked on at the encyclopedia company. Swimming was the finished product, there for the taking.

With each new stroke she took, all of the fragments and run-on sentences disappeared in bubbles that could be blown away, easy as child's play. She sharpened some always-hidden part of herself with every lap she counted, so unlike the sharpening of the sickly looking work pencil with the worn-out eraser on top, crumbling like she was crumbling, waiting for the death of the written word. She left behind her a flabby day of sitting, world without end, stuck in a cubicle, never having the time or energy to stand up and look out a window. Besides, that window was at least a hundred yards away from her desk; that felt like a mile once she had planted herself in her seat like a weed in the ground.

Now, she let irregular verbs slip through her wet fingertips along with cerebral references to the wisdom, or lack thereof, of the Civil War; head counts of Jews dying at Auschwitz; and George Orwell's use of euphemism in his book 1984. The content and soul of history and literature had become lost in the vacancy of her eyes, eyes that always mirrored back to her the need to look at something new, something bright.

One day her work provided an opportunity to proofread a story about Marie and Pierre Curie discovering radium. The surprise of their discovery surprised her as well. For a brief moment, she liked her job, but then she found some misspelled words, two unnecessary commas, an omitted semi-colon, and a series of unacceptable one-sentence paragraphs. A cancer of unclear language and lack of continuity circled the Curies as she kept imagining them dressed in black, sharing a perhaps restrained love for each other, standing in an austere environment near a half-eaten hard-boiled egg or yesterday's cup of leftover coffee.

She knew that she was a leftover as well, passed by in piles of other people's resumes and cover letters until she finally landed on the door steps of the encyclopedia company half by accident and half on purpose. This random thought now made her swim with purpose. Extend those arms further and push! Kick harder. Avoid panting, if possible. Breathe only when needed. Swim faster by traveling underwater. Become the fish. She laughed a little at the unwitting comparison to the labor pains of a woman-about-to-give-birth imagery that had entered her mind: push, kick, to pant or not to pant, breathe. Noticing for a moment how this slowed her swimming down, she decided to meditate instead on the benefits of a beginning yoga class.

Monotony, sitting for hours, immobility—they made her feel like an ant trying to crawl uphill in molasses. *That* would have been what she wrote for *her* job description—far more honest than "must have a keen attention to detail and a Bachelor's Degree, preferably in English or journalism." With new energy for swimming now returning, she thought of the saccharine litany of one boring day followed by the next with clockwork predictability along with, for better or worse, her own perfect view of the clock from the place where she sat like a cat in a carrier, unable to meow. Perhaps the always broken air conditioning was not so bad after all, as the impetus to swim grew larger with each passing hour of the day. At work she felt thick, like a winter stew, as the heaviness of gravity pulled her farther and farther into her own bodily indentations of the too-welcoming chair. But here, swimming made her light, like the first few rain drops hitting the green earth but not saturating it. In her mind, she could both swim and fly, and her once opaque body now slowly turned translucent, followed by such an intense transparency that she knew she could live inside this new home of self.

As though she were dictating a memo to no one in particular, she described to herself how she rode the bus to work and often felt the sudden stops as she watched those standing around her struggle to maintain their balance. Crowds of them all hanging on to their umbrellas, water dripping first down their faces and then their arms. One day, in almost 100 percent humidity, an obese man with a cane lost all control and landed sideways on her lap, his cane missing her left ear by about a quarter of an inch, his legs dangling across those of the woman sitting next to her. Perhaps they looked like an unplanned *ménage a trois* to the lucky folks sitting across from them. No matter. She had once fallen right on top of her professor on the bus ride home on the very first day of class.

When work came yet again—the reading that would make words look like small, stale cookies or as pointless as the drops of rain standing on the noses of strangers on the bus—she knew that the words read would lose their meaning when scrutinized, looked at individually, proofread down to the most minute detail. Did she need a magnifying glass; a microscope; even, ridiculously, she knew, a telescope? She had become blind to the very thing that was the reason she had been hired in the first place—words! The inserts, the arrows, the "stets" showing up every now and then as an act of good will indicating that she could remove that word, that turn of phrase, out of her vision—presumably for good, as in right now until forever. So what was stopping her from ripping up an entire page of official hard copy encyclopedia property? Extraneous to all of these twists, turns, and gyrations of the human mind came her reliable, though messy, support system of strong coffee, doughnut crumbs, paper clips, ink pens, and miscellaneous slips of paper, some sticking on her desk in correlation with the day's humidity, some sticking to her arms every now and again like leeches.

But here in the pool, what some might perceive as monotonous and too repetitive, she felt such peaceful freedom immersed in water with just the right amount of chlorine in it, the right amount of sun in the sky, just enough wind to make her feel like a sailboat gliding away from the confines of the shore. Coupled with an absence of the clamor of words, no matter how silent and harmless they looked on the written page, she knew that she had arrived in her own heaven, one with her name, and only her name, written on it.

She had supposed that if she had really wanted to, she could break the water around her by earnestly doing breast strokes and butterflies. She could divide it into parts and make it splash up against the sides of the pool, defying all of the miscellaneous paper clips that refused to really connect her life together in any sort of welcomed fashion. She could jostle the water around her in the same way that she had been jostled around. Then, the water would release her just like the bus had; only this time she would not be a victim. She would not go down and down to the floor of the pool and blow bubbles frantically in an attempt not to drown. She would not stand at the bottom of the pool in chains that anchored her in one place for all time.

Instead, now finished with her laps, she sank down and down and felt her toes touch the bottom of the pool. She knew she had arrived after descending swiftly, magnificently, to a point where she could stand briefly, breathlessly watching the other legs and arms around her that all seemed to take a form, a shape, as if they too were going someplace that mattered. Then, floating to the top, she let herself be like an island that no one ever visited. Her body floated with no particular sense of direction—partially up, partially down, partially sideways. Not only did this feel acceptable to her; it felt great, because at work she was pushed and pulled by her boss and the mounds of paper on her dusty desk. Sometimes she felt tossed in different directions simultaneously until there was nothing of personality left but a fragment or a sentence left hanging somewhere in mid-murky thought that might be turned into good prose only with abhorrently exhaustive effort.

After one last deep water submersion, with effort, she pushed the water down forcefully, in charge of each new step she took to get to the surface, reaching the dividing line between herself and the world, surprised at how long she had gone without taking a breath. She tread water for a while and watched the sun temporarily lend her its hue. Quivering in the water for a few seconds, she moved cautiously to the shallow end, not wanting anyone to bump into her.

As she stood in place to get out of the water, she made a mental note of what she wanted to experience in tonight's dream sleep, something that was impossible to see during the confines of the day: her body arched into a rough-ly ninety-degree ascent over the green earth as she swam and flew at the same time, surrounded by trees and flowers in full bloom on both sides of her, her feet having taken her last steps on earth, her arms outstretched to touch the first tantalizing revelation of the unknown world of shooting stars, creamy moonlight, and wind so soft that deep lake water around her held her inside its calm ripples as she entered a wordless place where even an urge to whisper would die in the angelic silence of this forever-precious night.

Looking for Home

I am white and small and decide to stand in the corner of the large living room of my house. Standing there quietly, I am hoping that the very architecture of my house will be sufficient to hold me up. These white stucco walls are much taller than I, and they have been here for over 100 years. I have inhabited this planet for only 28 years. When fall comes in a month, I will be 29, and someone will try to grab that year away from me.

The doors to my house are almost always open, and strangers come in and out against my will. I shout at them to leave, but no one listens to me. It is as though I must yell through a bullhorn to be heard at all, and even then, my voice sounds tiny and insufficient as my words drop to the ground like leaves.

I live by myself in this large two-flat on the first floor on the north side of Chicago. Momentarily, I leave my corner and walk out to the front of the building. The large frame of this house looks menacing and reaches the top leaves of tall trees. The exterior is gray and partly chipped. Since I have a cold and the humidity has been 90 to 100 percent for the past two weeks, I can hardly breathe. August has always seemed this way to me—a time for summer colds, the loud chirping of crickets, and cicadas that always sound as though they are mourning the impending loss of summer.

Grayer, my cat, stares out at me through the window. I must look funny to her standing alone, perspiration soaking my armpits, always coughing and trying to catch my breath. Every time I clear my throat it has to be cleared again.

The screen door won't shut tightly enough no matter how hard I slam it. Flies go buzzing in and out. Their noise thickens in the hot, moist air. It is 100 degrees today, tomorrow, yesterday, and all days before yesterday. All the flies seem changed—either immobile or dead as a result of their flight through air. How much am I like the fly, locked into a ridiculous stagnant faith that tomorrow will bring ice-cold relief?

I continue to stand outside, silent and pared down by this heat and my cold. The stranger is standing there again. I don't have to turn around and look at him; I can feel his presence. When I do turn around, I can see him dressed in khaki, grimy with dirt and sweat. Our eyes meet, a dialogue in its own silent right.

Gasping for breath, I run inside my house, but he is close behind me. He quickly grabs the dollar bills I have neatly stashed in to the back corner of my corduroy shorts pocket. Now, the money is his, not mine. I don't scream or yell for help or do anything to exercise my already weak vocal cords. Something has happened; something has changed just as the flies have changed.

This man keeps running in and out of my house, and the door sounds louder and louder to me each time it slams. He breathes evenly and steadily as though he is a regular man. I feel blood dripping from my Tampax into my panties, and I wonder if he can smell it as a shark might. I have been bleeding for almost two weeks now.

He runs through the screen door again, and this time I go with him. We look at my large, silent living room, so empty of furniture and noise. A grandfather clock on my wall ticks at a rapid pace, much faster than it should, the only sound.

More strangers are arriving now, buzzing in and out of my house, invading the corners, leaving empty spaces behind them. The walls become larger and whiter. I want to fight back, but it occurs to me that I need to bathe more than I need to do anything else. I go to the bathroom, turn on the faucet, and watch the water slowly fill the bathtub. Then, I return to the living room.

The strangers have all congregated there, refusing to enter any other room of my house. They are uniformly dressed in khaki, and there is not a woman among them. Their faces hold no expression—nothing happy or sad, depressed or lonely, determined or lethargic. They are mute, strong, and stiff as statues. Their abnormally large hands make my average-sized ones seem as tiny as a newborn's.

I have to leave the strangers to check on the water in the bathtub. When I walk into the bathroom, the tub has overflowed, and the cat is floating on its back, all four paws sticking straight up into the air. I have to walk through puddles to get to the animal and turn the faucet off. I keep turning the faucet, but it goes in circles, never coming to a complete stop.

Blood is coming through my shorts now, and Grayer will die if I don't get to her in time. I can't turn off the water, but why am I concerned about the water when my cat is dying right in front of me? My arms reach out to her, and it seems like such an effort to pick her up. I finally grab her, and at first it seems as though it is too late. Her body feels stiff and inflexible to me.

I have taken a course in cardiopulmonary resuscitation, and now I am wondering if what I know will work on a cat. She looks like a drowned musk-rat as I tilt her head back and give her a hard slap on her chest. Water runs from her nose and mouth. I put my hand on her belly, but I still can't feel her heart beat. Her paws look rigid and tired. I pry her mouth open, pull the tongue up to the roof, turn her over. Water pours from her mouth into the bathtub.

I hit her chest hard again, pull up an eyelid, and I know that I am seeing her return to life. My hand quickly goes to her heart again. Yes, it's there, that small, quiet murmur of a beat! Then, the most pathetic meow comes whimpering out of her throat. I grab her in my arms and hold her tightly, but then I immediately loosen up on her, not wanting to interrupt her breathing patterns. There is a small, almost imperceptible, movement of her tail.

The water keeps running, but it doesn't seem so important to stop it now. I bring the cat in to the living room, and the strangers are all gone. They have left behind them a large, almost empty, room. Where they stood, I see towering green plants.

I hear my sandals click against the hardwood floor as I carry the cat over to the window. We sit on the floor together. She is heavy on my lap, large and defenseless. I look down between my legs and see wonderful red menstrual blood dripping to the floor. A few flies hum in unison, and the noon sun invades my window, blinding my eyes.

I will nap long and hard with the cat, and when I dream, my fingers will be splayed against an airplane window, detached from the rest of my body. I might be on this plane taking off from O'Hare Airport, thankfully flying to a place much cooler than Chicago, and the earth will fall away from me in a large patch of green, then Lake Michigan, then a steady ascent. I will listen to silent conversations, be inside the minds of fellow passengers shaking their heads in disgust over the sloppy way the plane initially ascended. This will be followed by the echo of strangers walking down my broken front steps to street level.

A loud ticking of watches will reach a crescendo of deafening noise both on the plane and inside my Chicago apartment. I will listen for the first time to the city I live in, even in my panic when one siren's rail joins another and consumes all discordant noise. I will quiver like a candle's flame, my stature diminished.

Next to my stucco wall, I will stand until someone starts to pull on the strings of my marionette head. The room will grow larger into a brilliant white clarity that stabs my eyes as I pull the pillow away from my head to better hear several strangers earnestly knocking on my unlocked front door.

Then, I will awaken, be grounded in the transformation from August to September. The first thing I see will be the high ceilings of this room and I will know, not decide, if marriage and motherhood can fit inside my home.

Standing in the Dark with My Family

Twilight invades my house despite the early hour, through window panes etched with frost, through angled slats in half-closed blinds and the thread-thin cracks between the door and its frame. I have to go. Maggie will be fine. She's napping in her crib. She will be fine. I lock the door behind me, burying the nagging sense that I should stay. Well, I have no choice.

I run the first block, then the next. After a minute, an hour, a year, I am where I am going, my heartbeat a drum-beat in my ears, a thrum-beat, a metronome keeping time to the clock I know is ticking. Any second Maggie will wake, climb out of bed, tumble to the floor and…I run faster.

Once I finally push through the spotlessly clean glass doors of a bland office building, I see my fast-moving reflection in the glass. I'm a wreck—my cheeks ruddy and blotched, my long red hair emitting something akin to a corona, my psyche filtering through my abnormally erect body which now postures itself in preparation for a coronary.

No matter. I'm here to interview a babysitter for my daughter, a woman with excellent references. I talk to a man first who greets me at the glass doors. He says he will direct me to this woman. I see her in her small cubicle and note that she has a short black bob so unlike the chaos of my bright hair now dripping with sweat.

The man walks back to his cubicle, and I walk over to the woman's cubicle and sit across from her as if I will interview her. Another woman, as faceless as I sense I have become, sits next to the woman with the short black hair. Is she this woman's sidekick, or is she too striving to get a babysitter? Each clicking second of time cries out to me to grasp its elusive nature with both of my hands.

I try to talk with the woman with the short black hair, but she is busy. I force myself to take notes, but I don't know why. In the process of jotting things down, I decide to write an article about this organization, one for which

I used to do freelance writing. While taking notes, I discover my favorable impressions of the place, my good memories of the past.

Still, I cannot get information about the black-haired woman. She's too distracted, enmeshed in her work. I walk to the man's cubicle and ask him to check out her personnel file for me. He proceeds with my wishes, and every second feels like a minute, every minute an hour.

File doors open and close. The black-haired woman looks so efficient that she could be at a business meeting with one person, herself. My hope is that if I can get her attention, she will be as present for me as I would be for her. The man returns with a folder holding documentation confirming that the black-haired woman has excellent credentials.

I continue taking notes and realize I have the makings of a good article that I did not plan on writing. I came here for one purpose, now slowly morphing into another. The black-haired woman smiles at me with forced patience in her eyes. Our eye contact feels as brief as the kiss my husband gives me at 6:00 a.m., the workday already on his lips, one hand opening the door to a world he does not want to enter.

I keep looking at the woman frantically, then avert my eyes and see that business is as usual here: fast-paced, focused, oblivious to anything that does not appear on a computer screen. I try to swallow my agenda but choke on it instead.

My eyes turn to the black-haired woman again. Never have I seen such precision. Flawless black hair, not a strand of gray. Her red lipstick is smooth, moist, and shows no sign of fading. Each one of her eyelashes is distinctly separated from the others, and none of her mascara is caked. In fact, it looks as though it was put on five minutes ago. The eye shadow is deep lavender, in perfect harmony with the white of her face. Plucked eyebrows. No freckles, no age spots. Just costume skin she must have applied to her face right before she did her eyes.

My eyes then move to the perfect angles of her face that end in a square jaw line. Then, the white neck adorned by the elegance of a motionless silver necklace hanging over the symmetrical beginnings of cleavage. Large breasts, but not excessively large. I am stilled, motionless in my gaze.

I can't bear to let my eyes rest on her breasts and surely not her small waist. Instead, I find myself looking at one of her wrists where a silver watch gleams so intensely that I want to shut my eyes. Her watch has no second hand, not even a minute hand—no concern for time gone by in small doses.

Time runs out. My eyes drop to her feet at home in five-hundred-dollar shoes that match her lavender suit with businesslike precision. My heart races: where is my vaunted clarity?

Now, I remember Dorothy in *The Wizard of Oz*, her fatalism as she looks at the last few grains of sand slipping through the hour glass, knowing that she will die once the last grain of sand slips through unless she is rescued. I give up on time, give up on getting the information I need.

Shortly, after I dash out the glass door, I pretend that my harsh departure rattled the glass enough to break it into tiny pieces. This provides a measure of comfort when all the notes I have taken dissolve into thin dripping black ink that becomes a small river that trickles through my shoulder bag and begins to seep onto my unshaven legs. Everything adds up to the accuracy of a bank statement: I should not have left Maggie. I am a bad mother.

Now I must go through an obstacle course to get home to Maggie. I am agile. I race through hills and valleys and deal with bramble bleeding the life out of my legs, my sanity temporarily saved by the pungent pleasures emanating from raspberries and roses in a garden I don't have the time to enter.

I start climbing a hill when I spot a band of Eastern European people moving as slowly as molasses poured from jar to baking dish. They look like caricatures of ethnicity the closer I get to them. The women wear long black and red skirts and white blouses with puffed up sleeves and dance in a single row, their bodies stick straight, polished black heels adorning their invariably small feet. Their necks and wrists are almost impossible to see through the silver and gold necklaces and shimmering ruby bracelets. The men look as stiff as starched shirts from the waist up and wear perfectly ironed black pants and shiny black shoes. All of them are playing violins and occasionally exchange tentative flirtatious smiles and eye contact with the women.

Once the women stop dancing and the men playing the violin, they become lethargic and stand in two rows—one for women, the other for men. Unblinking eyes stare at me from faces still as mannequins. I cannot get past their uniformity, their solid stance on the hill. I keep running, almost stepping on their heels, breathing on their backs. I want to shove them out of my way, but instead politely discharge them from my presence with a flick of my hand. Soon, the sand will be stilled in the hour glass. I must get home.

I run uphill, downhill; next I catapult myself across a river. I should not have left Maggie, plain and simple. My running becomes frantic, insane, superhuman, and yet I still cannot run fast enough. I am also a robot, partially programmed to slow down but incapable of doing so. Zombie-like, I reach out for protection amidst ill-marked paths—no left, no right; no north, no south—just a continuous aimless circle. Silent children stand near me, and only some of them have faces. Seeing how stationary they remain, I run with magic and terror in my feet over a landscape I am seeing for the first time.

Finally, I sense my house appearing as if through a fog. I squint my eyes in the hope that I will see something familiar and safe. No more than an hour has passed since I left, so I try to comfort myself, knowing that Maggie almost always naps for two hours. A new, more-debilitating terror lodges itself in my unwaking body: I have been running for miles, for years.

Apprehension, sweat, conviction. I cannot recognize my own house. Everything is white and bland. Before I can see the evidence, I know that someone broke in. I see hallways with all the doors open, their hastily discarded locks on the floor.

My house has been turned upside down and me with it, and I know someone is standing in the hallway before I see him. A man's head is sticking to the ceiling, dark eyes that invade my hazel ones, both of our legs dangling uselessly as if we had been hung.

Shadow. Judgment. My father. When he comes into better focus standing next to an open door, not quite blocking it, I see he wears a wrist watch with thick black human hair glued to the places where his watch ends and his skin begins. Motionless in his business suit, he looks more like an artifact than a man.

"It doesn't look good," his monotone voice and strict face announce.

"What is it?" I ask.

"There's a baby in there," he presses on with an edge of despair. He could be referring to Maggie although she is a toddler and not a baby. "She is covered with blood." His voice flattens to that of a newspaper reporter, a small glimpse of necessary sympathy in his eyes.

My father then fades away from me, returning to the fog I try to see through in order to get home. The moment he fully disappears, I am struck with the desire to give my husband dark red roses, but then I see my father replaced with three men in gray suits, all of them seven feet tall with Nazi smiles pasted on their white lips. Puppet eyeballs begin to extend from their faces as I fix my gaze on them. They stand in front of a gate far shorter than they are. Once I look down to their combined six feet, I see they have all been stuffed into one large shining black patent leather boot. They are both dead and alive to me as they wink at me from the dangling sockets of doll eyes. I close my own eyes for a second. When I open them, their eyes return to their sockets as their barbaric smiles grow larger, showing huge polished white teeth.

<hr>

Bells from beautiful ancient clocks with ornate carvings of dragons meshed into cherry wood begin their sonorous announcement of a new hour of the day. I slither with the efficiency of a long black snake out of the clock and onto the comforter on my bed.

Finally awakening to the shadow of the house I call my own, I gently rock my husband Jack's shoulders back and forth but cannot hide the urgency in my voice. Soon after he wakes up, I learn that he too had a startling dream.

We talk. In his dream we are spiders, though our bodies have human forms. We are at his parents' house having sex when his father lifts up the blanket covering us to make sure that his son is not having sex with me in *his* house, in *his* bedroom. It makes no difference that we are married.

I am the male spider, Jack the female spider. I am aggressive. Jack likes this and wants to have sex with me but can't. I am replaced by another sexless male spider, a good spider that does not have sex. Jack warns his father that I can easily crawl back as spiders can slip underneath locked doors.

We crawl back into the net of each other's arms and laugh at the absurdity of spiders, at the slow band of Eastern Europeans blocking my way. We laugh at the danger of the large numerals 4:15 a.m. on the face of the alarm clock and the menace in my tangled nightgown that I pulled above my waist before I fell asleep.

I walk with unfounded trepidation into Maggie's room and listen to her quiet, steady breathing, the unfitful dream sleep of a child lost in timelessness. She does not yet toss in and out of terror as I stand there in the dark, looking at her, envying her safety in the twilight of my own crossing over between dreaming and wakefulness.

Perhaps I appear as a shadow in her dreams as I walk barefoot in and out of her bedroom, a guest in my own home still looking for something as precise as the woman with the black bob; for an hourglass holding precious time, not permitting the sand to slip through it.

I run my hand across Maggie's forehead, check for a fever, kiss her un-blemished skin. She stirs briefly as I close her bedroom door behind me. I feel the whisper of her breath as I stand silently for an unhurried moment, alert as a sentinel, before I return to bed, still eyeing the closed door. Surely, it might swing open before dawn takes its time to grace my family with another day.

Listening to Mozart

I get off the crowded Chicago bus and run through the snow, the exhaust fumes from the bus making it harder for me to breathe. Sweat drips down my back as I am wearing too many layers of winter clothing to be running in the cold. My pace quickens; my heart beats faster. I pump my way through city traffic and falling snow, wondering why I am so terrified of being five minutes late for your memorial service.

When I arrive, I discover I haven't missed a thing. I gasp for breath while I remove layers of clothing and wipe snow off my hat and hair. I catch my reflection in a mirror; my face is dark red.

I immediately discover the wisdom in my concern about missing even a minute of the service. Because you were cremated, your body isn't here. Instead, a huge bouquet of flowers reminds us of your life and death. There are no speeches, poems, canned organ music, or a minister who barely knew you, testifying to what a great person you were. Instead, we all humbly sit in hard-backed chairs to listen to Mozart for half an hour. *"Requiem aeternam dona eis, Domine, et lux perpetua luceat eis."* The Latin takes me out of the present, out of myself, into some shining perpetual light. No one seems ashamed to cry or wail, or not to. You are with us, and without us, in the Mozart.

I return a book you lent me to your sixteen-year-old daughter, Heather, and both of us laugh at the awkwardness of my gesture. She looks remarkably pretty in her wool-crepe dress and artfully applied eye makeup. Perhaps composure is her way of responding to death.

"Recordare Jesu pie, quod sum causa tuae viae, ne me perdas illa die." Remember, blessed Jesus, that I am the cause of thy pilgrimage; do not forsake me on that day.

Ovarian cancer. Dead at forty-six, eleven years older than I am. I remember the first time I met you: I was fourteen and you were my freshman English teacher. Students made fun of you because you left an entire set of our papers at the grocery store, failing to return them to us on time. One boy said that you wore a stupid gray dress with a red racing stripe down the middle of it. You heard all of this and more and were gracious enough to remain considerate of all students' feelings. We complained about late papers and jeered at your red racing stripe, never bothering to see that you graduated from Harvard, that you were brilliant, that you were preparing us very well for college.

Twenty years passed with no contact between us. Then, by coincidence, we both ended up teaching English at the same college. When I called you, you eventually remembered me and said you felt like a dinosaur once you recalled when you had me in class. We saw each other occasionally and entered that gray area between acquaintances and friends. You were someone I wanted to know better.

When I first heard of your cancer, I responded with phone calls, kindness, gifts, sensitivity. I tried to keep my own terror private and conjured up all sorts of "reasons" for your disease. You were teaching six classes at four colleges because you needed the money for you and Heather after your divorce. Therefore, you didn't get enough sleep. You didn't have a Pap smear for ten years. I heard my critical thoughts as if they came from the medical police.

Your former husband told you he would leave if you didn't quit your full-time teaching job. You believed him, at least long enough to quit a job you really liked. I remember that by the time you quit, you were comfortable enough with your students to go out for coffee with them. I've pegged your ex-husband as a total jerk who thinks women shouldn't have careers. If it weren't for him, you might have had one full-time job, not four part-time jobs. Am I mad at you for quitting? Would he really have left you? Maybe his absence, at least then, would have been more painful than losing your job. Who am I to say? The horrible irony is that eventually you were without both a husband *and* a full-time job.

Like a lot of other people, I'm taking a cause and effect approach to disease. By eliminating the cause, we can eliminate the effect. If I put each piece of the puzzle of the origins of cancer in the right place, I'll get the complete picture, the answer to why you had cancer and I have health. I really cared about what happened to you and I think you knew this, but in hindsight I wonder if you somehow heard my thoughts.

You struggled with the discipline of maintaining a macrobiotic diet that was, at least, giving you more time and reducing your suffering. I ran into you at an ice cream shop and couldn't hide my alarm when you ordered ice cream, a big no-no in a macrobiotic diet. What was I thinking? One scoop of ice cream and it would be the end of you? I also didn't hide my relief when you told me you were eating ice cream because you lost too much weight on the macrobiotic diet; you were eating it for the "right" reasons.

❦

We walked to your apartment in summer sunshine, your head wrapped in a scarf to cover your hair loss. You struggled up three flights of stairs to your apartment with a cane because you only had one lung.

Once inside your apartment, made spotlessly clean through the kindness of others, we talked about my upcoming wedding. You were concerned that you hadn't bought me a shower gift, and I, of course, wondered how you could even think of a gift at a time like this. As if having cancer should mean you suddenly have no interest in others.

You waxed poetic about going to Athens and Rome, saying this might be the last summer of your life. Our voices seesawed between humor and the recognition of your impending death. You went to Athens and Rome; it was the last summer of your life.

You then told me of a man you adore, how recently you made love with him and your wig fell off. You had panicked and covered your head with your hands. He removed your hands and caressed your baldness. Tears stood out in my eyes despite my efforts to control them.

When I left, I hugged you and was surprised by what I felt. Had I studied my medical textbooks well enough? Could I catch cancer from you? I was being ridiculous, so I didn't let my thoughts out in body language or words. Once in your arms, there was a part of me that didn't care if I "caught" cancer. I stood there idiotically paranoid and ashamed, but I'm at least glad that we touched each other.

We passed briefly in and out of each other's lives, the way people do when they know each other better than superficially but less than well. I know that you had been in and out of hospitals, that you were an atheist who once tried to believe in God. You gave up when you realized you were just faking yourself out. I wonder if there is any difference in the way an atheist and a believer approach death. I have no answers and not enough comfort, just the knowledge that belief in God is a necessity for me. I'm glad I'm not worried about the fate of your soul the way some believers would be. If I am wrong and there is no God, then maybe there is no soul. If I'm right and there is a God, then you're in heaven or at least a place of peace.

You once told me that you thought death was just like going to sleep but never waking up. If that's the way that you wanted it to be, I hope that's what it was for you.

❧ ❧

In mid-December, I was fired from my job. The dismissal was untimely and unfair. I hysterically smashed glass all over my kitchen floor. I gave myself one day to recover, and then I called you. I don't know if I called for the right reasons. Perhaps I felt that misery loved company or that I tried to put my pain in perspective by realizing that yes, I was jobless, but no, I was not lifeless.

But I didn't have the opportunity to listen once again to your fears, your regrets, your hopes. Maybe you would have cared that I had been fired from a job as you cared about the shower present. I don't really know what dying people care about. I try to single them out as the special people they are, but how do I know whether or not listening to other people's problems makes them feel connected to life, less concerned about and fearful of death? How do I know if I've talked too much about my own problems? Did I dump on a person who does not deserve to be dumped on? Do people still want to give of themselves, still listen, even when they are close to death?

❧ ❧

When I called, with all of my questions still unanswered, Heather answered the phone. I asked for you, and she said that you had passed away. My voice trembled in response. Heather's young yet mature voice held no tremor when she informed me that death was a part of life. The repeated sharing of the news of her mother's death had probably taken all of the cracks out of her voice.

My misery increased when I hung up the phone. If I hadn't called, I wouldn't have had to deal with both a lost job and a lost friend. I also would never have had the opportunity to say goodbye to you at such a touching memorial service.

I entered Christmas as though I suffered from a sort of spiritual cancer. I exchanged gifts, went to parties, didn't look for jobs, and let people take holiday snapshots of me. My mother-in-law said that I didn't look like myself in these pictures.

Losing a job and a friend don't go well with Christmas. People expect us to force cheer at the holidays. When I told a distant relative that I was fired from a job one day and learned the next that a friend had died, she opined that the job never meant that much to me anyway. I responded to her amateur psychology by remaining politely and furiously silent.

After your memorial service, I walk slowly to catch the bus. The snow con-
tinues to quietly fall, and the moon is barely visible. I once again smell exhaust
fumes and my own sweat as I board the bus. It becomes darker and colder,
but a few stars promise to light up the sky as the Mozart bells peal in my ears,
telling me to remember, remember, remember.

In memory of M.D.

Lovely Invasion of Soul

"Those who sing pray twice."
St. Augustine of Hippo

One day I was not a dedicated singer. The next day, and all days after that, I was.

About nineteen years ago, another mother of a seven-year-old and I were chatting it up in the gym where our daughters were playing some version of beginning basketball. We sat on the risers, laughed a lot; and for a few precious moments, we "de-mothered" each other with adult-to-adult talk and little or no interference from seven-year-old girls. Then, out of exhaustion and silliness, we started to lie down on top of the risers, pretending that we were in our own little world, perhaps attending some version of an adult slumber party.

Although we had no blankets to cover ourselves and get cozy, for a good ten minutes we put our forty-something selves on hold, as we had no doubt about their return. My friend Greer began talking about how much she loves musicals, *The Sound of Music* in particular. I put in a vote for *West Side Story*, a movie I had first seen at least twenty-five years ago. I recalled bits and pieces from the song "Tonight," perhaps because I once sang a solo of it as a terrified fourteen-year-old. I started speaking some of the words out loud, and Greer listened attentively. Once I was confident my remembrance of "Tonight" did not seem too far away from the actual song lyrics, I began to sing: "Tonight, tonight, won't be just any night. Tonight, there will be no morning star." Then, I mumbled a bit in semi-forgetfulness and eventually called up some of my favorite lines: "Oh, moon, grow bright and make this endless day endless night." Soon, I realized I was probably too close to the end of the song and backpedaled to "Today, the minutes seem like hours, the hours go so slowly...."

Greer congratulated me on my musical prowess, and then I listened to her abbreviated version of "My Favorite Things": "Raindrops on roses and whiskers on kittens, bright copper kettles and warm woolen mittens, brown paper packages tied up with strings, these are a few of my favorite things."

Then, she paused as she tried to remember the next verse. She sang "Cream-colored ponies and…." I filled in the blank for her and sang for all I was worth "Crisp apple strudels. Doorbells and sleigh bells and…." Greer chimed in with a bit less volume "schnitzel with noodles." We paused for a moment, and I said, "You know, we really ought to sit up if we are to sing right! We might remember the words a bit better that way too!"

We stared at each other for a few seconds after we changed the position of our bodies. "Isn't this great!" we both said at almost the same time. Greer requested that we start singing the rest together. "Yes, yes," I practically shouted, some teenage glee beginning to filter into me from the waist up and getting stronger and stronger until I said "one, two, three" in a now loud and powerful singing voice followed by "Wild geese that fly with the moon on their wings, these are a few of my favorite things," and we were mainly together, and we mainly didn't care if we weren't.

"Let's quit while we are ahead, okay?" I gasped.

"You know, Margie, you have a really good voice!"

"Oh, you have to be kidding. I haven't sung in years." I felt rather modest and charming at the same time. Maybe now I could be that girl in a white dress with blue satin sashes and ride off into the sunset on a pony while eating crisp apple strudels! After all, Mark Twain did once famously say that he could live for two months on a good compliment.

Greer and I soon returned to motherhood and all its chronic responsibilities. But I caught myself humming: "When the dog bites, when the bee stings, when I'm feeling sad, I simply remember my favorite things, and then I don't feel so bad" as the two of us and our two children exited the gymnasium with *The Sound of Music* and *West Side Story* now embedded inside of us, and we both felt a good twenty years had been instantly stripped away.

Usually I would just be happy with a compliment as sincere and free of empty flattery as I knew Greer's comment was, but something began to stick in my head. As I let my past crawl into my present as we walked out of the Broadway Armory in Chicago to get back in our cars and drive home, we hugged and I said, "Don't you just wish you were still sweet sixteen?"

Greer laughed and said goodbye to my daughter Maggie and me. I picked up Greer's daughter Maya and held her in my arms just as long as I would my own child, since I had babysat her off and on, and she felt like a second child to me. Sunlight still ruled the day, the traffic was strangely light for early evening rush hour traffic, and in that one moment before we put our cars into drive, Greer and I were still young and perhaps on our way to dancing all night to the music in our hearts.

※ ☙

A week or so passed, and I found myself thinking about singing almost every day. First I only sang in the shower or while listening to radio songs. Then I would start daydreaming after Maggie went to bed, rolling all the way back to when I was maybe in third grade. I remembered overhearing a music teacher telling my mother that I really should be getting voice lessons. Next came singing "There's a Song in the Air" as a soloist for a Christmas pageant when I was a senior in high school and singing soprano in the Glenview Community Church choir. I remembered singing *a cappella* in the Glenbrook South High School Choir and the day I unwittingly soloed when the conductor requested that only the red-headed sopranos sing! I kept looking around in a daze trying to figure out which I should be the more self-conscious of—my red hair, now inviting the stares of five or six boys and two blond girls, or my voice that, once I became aware of it, sounded somewhere south of angelic and north of terrified.

Then I fast forwarded to singing in the Oratorio Chorus in undergraduate school at the University of Iowa. After college, most of my singing life lay dormant for almost ten years, with the exception of occasional Sunday morning church singing. I started taking voice lessons in my early thirties, both in Chicago and Denver, the city I moved to for a year. Once, when no auditions were required, I sang in the Colorado Music Festival in Boulder, Colorado. The chorus and orchestra performed one of Mahler's symphonies outdoors with the Rocky Mountains rising behind us and sunlight slowly drifting into sunset. It felt as though Ravinia in Highland Park, Illinois, had been transported to the Rocky Mountains!

Before the first movement began, when twilight had not yet fallen, the aroma of lilac permeated the air. I heard the violins and cellos warming up and sensed the color of the sound. I foresaw that the chorus and orchestra would bloom that night and that by concert's end darkness would descend upon the moon's flight to heaven.

When the concert ended with startling applause and a slight summer breeze in the air, I walked carefully across the risers. I had been in a back row, being taller than most of the other sopranos. Before my feet touched the now dark grass that had just a little rain on it, I turned to look at the Rocky Mountains, so still and quiet in the midst of our singing. In my own stillness, I saw a shooting star streak across the northern sky and slip behind a mountain. I had no breath or voice when my feet reached the earth. Then, the full moon appeared, providing me with a dim light as I walked alone down a path lined with tall calla lilies swaying like dancers in the now stronger breeze. I saw my fiancé looking for me and we found each other under the stars.

❧ ❧

This symphony experience stayed in my mind for the entire time I lived in Denver, more vivid than any other musical memory I had. Before I moved back from Denver to Chicago, so that my future husband Jim and I would not be in a commuter relationship forever, I auditioned for the Denver Symphony Chorus. I even took several voice lessons first and, although I did not make it into the chorus, I did make the alternate list for sopranos, ranking number ten out of forty alternates. I considered that to be a minor trophy at the time.

So here I was, back in Chicago and now in the tenth year or so of a singing drought, and I found myself aching to be a part of a choral group again. The shower singing just did not cut it anymore. But every now and then, when I felt bold and lacking in self-consciousness, I would walk down the street on hot summer nights, first only thinking of such lyrics as "I have often walked down this street before, but the pavement always stayed beneath my feet before." Then, I would start singing the lyrics and, well, if I did run into a passerby, or worse still someone I knew in the neighborhood, at least it was dark. Besides, Chicago summer nights almost beg for music, improvised or otherwise. Every long-term resident of Chicago who has dealt with a Chicago winter savors each summer night sitting on a porch or swimming in Lake Michigan past dusk, and we don't turn our noses up at good guitar playing or song or dance on the street either.

So, several more voice lessons later, I auditioned for what is now the temporarily, if not permanently, defunct Choral Ensemble of Chicago. My mediocre -to-average sight-reading skills felt like a barrier to me and were likely the major reason I did not advance further in the Denver Symphony Chorus auditioning process. I had to hide how startled I was when the conductor told me that the ability to sight-read music was not all that important, that I had a good ear, and that he wanted me to sing in the chorus. That was joy, of course, but what followed was one singer's version of baptism by fire. I hung in there for a good long time and enjoyed much of what we sang, but I felt at times that I was draining both my vocal cords and my spirit. The conductor, while full of enthusiasm and some of the wildest eccentricity I have ever been privy to witness, was the most abusive conductor I have ever known. He would yell at us for no good reason with shocking regularity. I felt less alone when a tenor, also a psychiatrist, mentioned to me that the air in our practice room was filled with toxins. How sad, I thought, in my naiveté about the strange breed of choral conductors. I hoped my love of singing could withstand what was fast turning into a raw fear of even showing up for rehearsals. I finally saw that I was more dreading than looking forward to attending rehearsals of an all-volunteer chorus.

I finally got the courage to quit that choir, with no way to fill the hole in my spirit. I felt that quitting was my way of promising myself that, yes, I would get into another choral group. And, yes, I did.

I auditioned for the North Shore Choral Society of Evanston in 1996 for the second soprano section and got in after sitting through the bulk of a rehearsal listening to the fine sound of this chorus. The sweet second soprano section leader told me during a break that she knew I would get into this chorus. That kindness and faith in me coming from a total stranger...well, it did not hurt my fragile ego.

The rehearsal ended, and I walked up to the conductor, Dr. Donald Chen, with determination, terror, enthusiasm and "let's get it over with" written all over my face. I did not know what to expect. Sometimes choral conductors are so busy they don't have time for audition niceties. Donald warmed up my voice for a minute, then played intervals, and had me sing the intervals back for him. In no more than three minutes, the audition was over, Donald smiled at me, and said, "You're in!" No sight reading or singing an entire piece. God is good.

Beaming like a young girl, I walked over to the kind second soprano section leader, whose name I learned was Anne. I did not even have to say a word, and all she said was "I told you so!" Something about this woman suggested that we might become friends for life. Shaking, happy, exhausted, I left the hall where the rehearsal took place at the Unitarian Church in Evanston and wondered what it would be like to sing with 120 to 160 singers, a much larger group than the small choir I had left behind.

With the exception of a few missed concerts due to my husband's work schedule, I have sung in most North Shore Choral Society concerts since 1997. I have a humble approach to my singing, and with each new choral task over the years I have continued to be slightly stunned when I find myself singing better than I thought I could. I have come to realize that, for no logical reason, I am the kind of singer who thrives when other singers believe in my talents more than I do. Apparently that belief rubs off on me, incrementally increasing my belief in my own singing voice.

Years after I joined the choir, the North Shore Choral Society got word that the chorus would be singing at the Ravinia Festival in Highland Park, Illinois. The thrill of this good news was palpable the night we all learned of it. Still, the stage at Ravinia would not hold all of our 160 singers, so there had to be something akin to auditions. Some people had schedule conflicts, shrinking the pool of available singers. The pool of singers went down again as some members resisted auditioning. I fought it right up until the last seconds before I did it. None of us had a clear idea what Donald was looking for. I heard a crack in my voice when I sang for him, apologized for it, and kept on singing, all the while thinking, "Well, nice try, Skelly, but you have surely blown this one big time!" I only heard the sound of my voice ringing loudly in the room.

Finished with the audition, which happened right before one of our practices, I let myself fall into my usual routine of self-talk: *Well, you know you didn't make it. I mean how could you after that one unforgivable shriek? Heavens, this is Ravinia, and you are not a professional singer. How crazy are you to even audition in the first place? Just look at all of those other people in the chorus who were wise enough not to waste the conductor's time with an audition. Why, they self-selected themselves right out of what they knew was a lost cause. But not you. You had the sheer chutzpah to audition, no matter what you sounded like.*

A rehearsal or two later, of course, curiosity got the best of me when I heard that the results of the Ravinia audition were now in the hands of the section leaders. I should at least phone Anne to confirm that I could not possibly have gotten into that select group of people who were singing at one of the most famous music venues in the world. Still, I heard that small hopeful voice inside of me and told her to take leave of me with her insidious ill-founded optimism.

Anne shuffled through some papers on the other side of the phone while I told her I just knew I did not make it. "I could have sworn I saw your name on that sheet, Margie."

"Are you kidding me?" Even worse than not getting picked for Ravinia would be erroneously thinking for a minute that I actually did get picked and then learning that I did not.

"Oh, Margie, you put yourself down too much." I heard more shuffling of papers and contained my eagerness, hope, despair, and self-denigration, thinking that I might pop out of my own skin. "Okay, I have the sheet in front of me. I'm looking at your name right now. You made it."

"Oh, my God, oh my God. Holy cats, you're sure?"

"No, I made it up!" Then, Anne's laughter was so convincing that I felt all doubt evaporate.

We savored the moment a bit longer and then I said to Anne, "You know, it was not all self-denigration that made me think I would not pass the audition. There was one place when my voice cracked noticeably, enough so that I apologized to Donald."

"I bet Donald did nothing more than smile briefly at you and provide you with the body language or a word or two to encourage you to keep on singing."

"Is he not the nicest conductor on the face of the earth?" Then, the tears of both appreciation and relief came unbidden. "Sorry, Anne, but this just means so much to me!"

"You could have fooled me!"

A few months later, and there we all were on the Ravinia stage for rehearsals. I loved being outdoors singing again, and I sensed that although it was a lot of hard work, we blended well and exuded the enthusiasm appropriate to what we were singing.

A few other like-minded souls practically gasped when *A Chorus Line* composer Marvin Hamlisch took the podium, baton in hand, for our first, perhaps only, rehearsal with him. Was I hallucinating? No, there he was, standing right in front of us in his black suit with a huge smile on his face. We all broke into spontaneous applause and then worked our voices into a state of near exhaustion. It was worth every moment, every mistake that was eventually rectified, every fleeting moment of self-doubt. Hamlisch proved to be a funny man, both at rehearsals and during the performance, and downright kind and encouraging—so much so that he even announced to the audience, "How about this great chorus?" Their applause affirmed his enthusiasm for our singing.

As always, with almost any concert I have sung in, unpredictable things happened. The stage lights were so bright that I could barely make out the first row of the audience, much less the rows behind them. Then, I realized what a huge gift this was for me, as it reminded me of the time I sang a solo in the Glenview Community Church when I was a senior in high school. The entire church was cast in darkness, and the only sound came from my voice and the organ. I could not see anybody, and nobody could see me. One small reading light illuminated my music score. My inability to see the audience or be seen by them boosted my confidence.

Perhaps all of us were in the musical equivalent of a sports marathon, one in which the end of the concert constituted the finishing line. In the midst of most concerts I have sung in, I vacillate between being present in the moment and thinking, "Don't worry. This concert will be over soon!" Singing, for me, at least concert performance singing, feels like walking on a tightrope, but one on which others have my back as I do theirs.

I have developed a self-talk that for the most part works for me and makes singing spiritually meaningful as well. I tell myself that my singing no longer belongs to me but has been transformed into a gift for the audience. I also tell myself that I cannot bide my time in a concert performance. Unlike when I write poetry, when it seems I have countless opportunities to get it right (the latter suggesting that there could possibly ever be a bona fide "rightness" in the first place), concert singing feels to me like something akin to riding a dangerous roller coaster, only because the roller coaster takes you on a ride you cannot control. Likewise, in a chorus I have no control over the other singers, the conductor, the orchestra, or the audience. I give my voice away and it is taken over by the conductor, who somehow, miraculously and magnificently, brings form, order, and zest to a large group of singers.

Once I heard that the North Shore Choral Society, while not as huge as the Mormon Tabernacle Choir, was described as a giant semi-truck that had to be pulled and tugged to get it moving in the right direction. If we hang our heads out of the windows of that semi-truck, if we fall asleep at the wheel, if we are not constantly aware of the "traffic" of other singers, violins, cellos, clarinets, trumpets, drums, and the piano, then we greatly increase the odds of us having an accident.

❧ ❧

For me, the highlights of singing with North Shore Choral Society include Bach's *Mass in B-Minor*, Handel's *Messiah*, Beethoven's *Ninth Symphony*, Mendelssohn's *Elijah*, and modern-day Morton Lauridsen's *Lux Aeterna*.

Bach's *Mass in B-Minor* has announced God to me in a way no other Mass, or for that matter any other church service, has. After singing it two or three times and seeing and hearing a live concert performance of it, I became aware that its length—close to 160 choral pages with 24-plus movements—does not to seem so long because this Mass affects me in somewhat the same way that Handel's *Messiah* does.

When I was twenty-four, I heard *Messiah* performed in Rockefeller Chapel at the University of Chicago in Hyde Park. Years later, when I was considerably older and had sung in several *Messiah* concerts, I often found myself remembering that day in Rockefeller Chapel. When almost everybody had left the church, I walked over to where the chorus had sung, standing there for what seemed like a long time, my sweating hand in the hand of a man I loved. We looked at each other and knew no words were necessary. I was standing on sacred ground and sensed the powerful way in which the earth had slipped away from my touch. I could in no way move my body. Heaven had invaded me, and no one tapped me on my shoulder or whispered the words "cliché experience" or "trite" in my ears. Through a stained glass window, I saw December snow fall to the ground, white glistening in sunlight; the fragile earth tried to accept this gift, and the wind in between the scattered flakes made this reception possible.

The soprano section of Beethoven's *Ninth Symphony* is so intimidating that I was in awe of any soprano who could sing the last movement without a crack in her voice. After singing the soprano section one time in concert performance, I questioned my sanity. Not only is singing in German a challenge, but doing it in the midst of many technically difficult runs—some of them jumping from one octave to the next, often at the high end of any soprano's range—made me think that Beethoven wanted real angels, not mere mortals, to sing his last movement.

For the Beethoven's *Ninth* concert, I screwed up my courage and asked Meister Chen if he would mind if, for this concert only, I became a first alto. He did not blink an eye when he complied. Imagine my surprise when two or three more timid sopranos joined in my defection.

That said, so much wonder, surprise, and joy live inside that *Ninth Symphony*...all the more when we consider that Beethoven was deaf when he wrote it, so never heard it performed. Doing the choral music justice seemed more fitting than ever, almost as though we singers could imagine Beethoven composing it in his own mind and soul but with no sound check for that mind and soul. And all of us got the fringe benefit of feeling as though we were actually attending a concert, not just singing in it, as so little of Beethoven's *Ninth* is actually choral.

Then, there is Mendelssohn's *Elijah*. I will always remember how frequently I listened to the overture in preparation for the choral section that followed. Trouble is that this particular overture never fails to bring me to tears, whether I am singing or listening, particularly in that brief startling moment right before the entire choir exclaims in full-force *forte*, "Help, Lord! Help, Lord! Help, Lord! Wilt thou quite destroy us?"

I often listen to that overture, an intoxicating breath of fresh air, while driving. I think there should be a warning on the cover of all *Elijah* CD's: "Do not attempt to drive a car, foul or fare weather, while listening to the overture! If you do take this risk, at the first sign of tears or a shaking body, you are directed to pull over to the side of the road, turn off the engine, and take several calming deep breaths. You are also advised to resist the urge to sing anything pertaining to the Lord, the end of both harvest and summer, or worse still, the notion that no power will cometh to help you...or for that matter, anybody else!"

Finally, the best way to get a sense of how I feel about Morton Lauridsen's *Lux Aeterna* is to read the poem I wrote about it in the poetry section of this book. That poem is titled "Sonnet in Praise of *Lux Aeterna*." I think only a poem can capture the sense of clarity this modern piece of choral ecstasy inspires.

Singing over these two decades has surprised me in ways I never could have imagined. Once I could drop my fears of being judged harshly by conductor, fellow singers, audience members, and most harshly by myself, I was sometimes able to sense real bonding and spiritual union with other singers. Some of us would admit to pushing back tears at the end of a concert while others, like myself, acknowledge that once the concert was over we didn't bother to block our tears. How very freeing to let tears be in charge and not some puffed up version of our controlling self.

At least twice I have sensed an overwhelming spiritual connection with an audience. In those moments at the end of Beethoven's *Ninth Symphony* and Bach's *Mass in B-Minor*, both performed in the presence of amazing acoustics at Pick-Staiger Concert Hall in Evanston, Illinois, time stopped. There was this space, however long or short, between the last breath of sound and the audience's first reaction to the entire concert—a space in which the power of the human voice and extraordinarily gifted instrumentalists suddenly, with no warning, broke down any barrier between audience and performers. The human soul could no longer hide; it was present everywhere: the semi-circle of choral singers dressed in black, the conductor's bowing, the stage lighting, and the entire orchestra visible to the singers as we stood on risers above them. The inevitable exhaustion that comes from both performing a difficult piece well *and* the audience's immersion in the transformative power of great music gave birth to something of palpable substance. No words do this experience justice, but the best words that I can come up with are these: the involuntary rising of an audience for a standing ovation becomes something far more precious than applause or appreciation. I caught myself trying to establish eye contact with some of these strangers in the audience. Their faces looked nothing less than radiant to me. Then, I knew more concretely why music has been called the universal language. The audience received the gift we bore, and with that, the notion of my single lonely self simply slipped away.

<hr />

At this writing, in May of 2015, I am looking forward to singing in the last North Shore Choral Society concert of the season, titled *Swing*. As far as I know, North Shore Choral Society has never offered such a great mixture of Swing, Big Band, Jazz, and Gospel.

Our first piece in the concert is titled "Sing, Sing, Sing" and announces to all of us—performers and audience alike—that "all you have to do is sing." That is such a wonderful way to put it, making singing sound easier than we think it is. And sometimes that really is true: singing can be easy and fun.

It was with this spirit that I decided in 2010 that I wanted to take on another chorus, the Edgewater Singers of Chicago. That entailed the newest conductor the organization had in its thirty-year history, Michael Oriatti, listening to our voices—perhaps scales and intervals. This had less of the feel of audition and more of him just getting to know each individual singer's voice. I joined this community chorus because I wanted something smaller, to be more accountable for my singing.

So, instead of singing in a second soprano section that had two dozen women in it, I was now one of only five or six second sopranos. One time at an Edgewater Singers Concert, my husband told me that he could actually hear my voice. Singing in this manner proved to be invigorating, fun, and as usual for me, terrifying.

Because the chorus remains small, at least compared with North Shore Choral Society, we knew each other well, and newcomers became acquainted in short order. There was a party after almost every singing rehearsal that included wine, good food, laughter, and engaging conversation—everything from jokes about the philosopher Descartes to politics and all things singing. Michael once told the chorus that singers tend to live longer than other people. I could not argue with that; nor did I want to.

Some people tell me that poetry saves lives, while others say that singing does the trick. Of course, both camps are right. I have at times been prone to mild-to-severe depression. Poetry provides an enduring compass, an aid in navigating personal struggles, giving me a way to hang my sadness on words instead of being victimized; to escape from a pervasive feeling of being locked inside an outrageously over-active mind, that, left to its own devices, might well spiral out of control. Singing with a group of people, on the other hand, transports me beyond that self to a place where the group is indeed greater than the sum of its individual parts. Who would have thought that discarding the self could result in so much happiness and joy? Happiness, temporary for most of us, has always baffled and evaded me. Laughter does not baffle or evade me, as happiness does, because laughter comes unbidden. For many of us, there seems to be more of a formula for achieving happiness than there is for laughter. Laughter seems to require no formula at all, praise be to God.

The lyrics of "Sing, Sing, Sing" move on to "Summer, fall, winter, spring, these are all good times to sing...."

Those who sing will invade your soul. So do poets. And you will consider both of them lovely company.

Part Three: Poems

Unpublished poets are still poets. We continue to write our poems, sometimes we submit them for publication, always we love them. My poems are about the ordinary in life: love, family, home, pets, and travel. Lots of travel.

So take a trip with me in which the sites you see are both familiar and foreign, pleasant and hard to look at. The journey begins with "The Gift of Trans-Atlantic Flight." Take-off has just passed, and you are good at estimating what might be going on in the minds of other passengers. Following this poem is a different kind of flight, taken after the Boston Marathon bombing.

From then on, you will meet all sorts of people, including a man intent on playing the guitar, an angel arriving at a train station, and two young strangers "struggling" to have sex on a train! How often do we read about affairs? My hope is that you will find an interesting twist in another poem in which sex and an affair refuse to show up at all!

The comfort and peace of finding home while taking a walk, visiting the California coastline, and sipping coffee in the early morning at camp appear in the poems "Walking the Path toward Home," "At Home," and "The Coffee Percolator on the Gas Stove."

As we travel further into the poetry, we witness Glacier National Park in all its majesty and color and the silent ordinary beauty of a train ride through Montana. Lightning "speaks for itself" in a train trip headed east of Denver. In another poem, a little girl waits for a train to arrive in "her very own station."

Falling in love, and staying in love, in some of these poems takes on mystery, terror, and variety. I pictured my dog falling in love with me as I am with him! Who knows for sure what goes on in the minds of our pets? I fell in love too with the North Woods night sky. I was at Chicago's Aragon Ballroom on the night my father, hindered by polio, found the courage to walk across the dance floor to ask my mother to dance.

These poems are filled with the innocence of children, particularly my own daughter, Maggie. They are filled too with the quest of adults. None of us is immune to tragedy and loss, and I have tried to discover the best words to treat death and suicide respectfully.

Finally, this collection of poems, which are now officially published, moves toward its ending with the poem "Passenger" and one about a group of people attending a Taizé prayer service. As I read these poems now, I realize the extent to which I rely on belief in God and a spiritual world that will forever both touch and elude us mortals.

My hope is that the poems will come full circle by the time the reader is finished with the final poem, "Winter Solstice." In "The Gift of Trans-Atlantic Flight" I write, "Angels breathe infinity on top of the rotating world." In "Winter Solstice," that same tired earth is "pulled by angels." May words always transform us poets, be the gift we both receive and give—the guardian angels that pull us softly and gently out of our very selves.

The Gift of Trans-Atlantic Flight

Angels breathe infinity on top of the rotating world
as we depart from one day and enter another;
earth-light shimmers—sun rising, setting; moonlight enters, disappears,
clouds slide underneath us, the engine faint as a whisper.

My fingers splayed against a naked thick, but tinsel window,
silent conversations, minds talking loudly, their pilot reassurance voices
ascend in crashing volume in the quiet of our ears,

in the leaving behind of parents, children,
even my pale glass reflection. The plane's slender wing
soon rests in sky and cloud, one light beaming at its end,
finger poised to touch stars.

Our plane lets the heavens own it, if only for a slipping moment,
as it breathes into ascent. Watches tick in unison, we—
supported by wings, wind, calm—fail with clock-like precision
to measure time's passage, this unopened present,
this gifted passage from shore to shore.

Flight after Marathon

Once again in dream sleep, I don't know who I am.
This time, bomb smoke dies in the hands of my eight-year-old, Martin,
who blows it out with the same ease he will use
to blow out nine candles on next year's birthday cake.

I roll over and become nine years old,
see already the gathering of dust on my tombstone
but can still make out the engraved Denise Richard,
followed by a row of blurred numbers.

Blindfolded I sense a damning dawn.
Even one ray of light promises me nothing
but my hands tied in back of me with rope.

Twin blackbirds grace my sky with eternal night flight
over Boston, and I, meshed in the glide of both, free my hands
to gather the stars, then infuse them with white.

Paps Sings the Blues

Paps—slow, fat, old—
loves me like no other man loves me.
He smells depression on me faster
than my husband smells sex
because depression is slow and relentless,
an old friend singing sorrow.

I run around a lot, fill up every minute of my day,
stay up nights to look for the moon but can't find it
and am always dripping from sex.
Then, comes dawn and work.

After tedium, I take a break with Paps,
He sings the blues, I drink coffee and laugh
when he sings about a rat race
and fingers with effort the strings
of his guitar to create fast.

The buzzer rings.
We rise, inch our way back
to our separate dust-filled factory stations,
work at becoming whole or just keep on working,
neither one of us seeing our limits:
the sex, the blues.

Etiquette for Former Chicago Lovers

Between Belmont and Diversey
on the Ravenswood train,
we order our past like a cup of coffee,
share the same seat for less than a mile
as strangers asking for a common courtesy
and graces most social, the aftermath of love.

Beyond a window, two birds circle each other,
their wings beating fast from the cold.
Soon we see only the sky
and are as grounded and common
as two spilled cups of morning coffee.

My Father Waits for Me

At bus stops, train stations, corner bars,
he grows impatient for a daughter
with no bus fare, no train schedule,
and closes an unfamiliar bar
at night, when it's late

when a distant gunshot opens the night
as the owl's unblinking eyes grow into stare
and a dog's barking is patient, persistent,
letting up for no one.

My father keeps his vigil,
a hound sniffing out its victim.
He waits and waits, a ticking clock,
but tick tock tick tock

two too late to ever come home.

Past the Stars

You come out of nowhere, announce your presence with wings.
Taxis, airplanes, trains—all the same: they don't bring you.

You're not from out of town. A taxi driver recognizes you—
someone he should have talked to on a starlit evening
while the tall buildings shot past him down the lake shore drive,
down the winding traffic heading furiously to the new city.

This journey is over. Desire wraps itself around my fingers.
The train moves involuntarily into the station past altitude, past experience.
You appear as something I couldn't even hope for,
and now as you pass through the gate,
you are the familiar stranger residing everywhere.

Your face maps the land you traveled—
    unseen mountains at night as you lay asleep
crunched in your seat like a paper doll
    as the train moved its way—slow, majestic,
arriving at an altitude of experience you couldn't have hoped for.

This starlit evening heads to the new city where you stand fluttering
and I recognize you for the first time as an unopened invitation.
I bring you to the tallest evening where the shore ends and traffic fades

like the last ray of sunlight slipping under the western horizon.
I bring you, unannounced, to this place. I move you.

The Same Night

A hug and a kiss and *I'll see you soon,*
We're off—you on your motorcycle, I on my train.

Still, even as we travel to different destinations,
the same night rises thin and bright above us.

Even now I can hear you gearing up,
wheels spinning against new pavement.

Even now we whisper to each other: *I see you see me soon.*
No language can separate us—no comma while we think

What to say next? No sentence of living in separate cities.
No question, we will write of all that remains of our thin skin,
    this driven night.

Strangers and Friends

On the night train headed west, I've left the sun behind in the time changes
as two strangers in front of me talk frantically through the night
trying to strip their time apart while I turn myself in and out of fitful rest,

listen to the pawing whisper of getting to know you,
    getting to know all about you.
He's twenty-five, she assures him that most of her friends are in their thirties
though she's nineteen. I'm assured of nothing but a bad night's sleep

and my way-past-thirty years. She likes doughnuts;
they both read the newspaper. She insists on eight hours of sleep a night
(I'm tempted to tell her to get it!) while he likes five.

And now that the night and train rest in quiet,
they steal the sex out of each other. I hear her familiar
suppressed panting; she is turned both on and off.

Then, the muted noise of opening and closing zippers
requires their thin laughter: the train light above their seat is still on,
so visible in my own dark. They exchange more odds and ends:

Will she eat scrambled eggs for breakfast? Will he eat a Danish?
I'd like something sweeter: the certainty of familiarity,
my place in the generation gap and eight hours of uninterrupted sleep.

As guardian and voyeur of their sex and mine, I have not once seen
their sharp free-love faces at dawn, and yet I know them,
strangers and friends bound for the West Coast...and so am I.

Anatomy of a Woman

Hair

Pull it back with your fingers, satin before sheets,
remember its color in dawn, in twilight.

Forehead

It appears as the beginning, the start
of the electric descent to her body.

Lips

Meet yours, man, a first impression,
so kiss her like a dancer—deft, deliberate, decisive.

Eyes

More than window panes or guides, reflections
of her ancestral seeing into childhoods of tomorrow.

Shoulders

Let your hands stop here. Pause,
like a comma, before you touch gold.

Whisper

Tonight's moon, not yet new. I am on top, giving you roses
as the curve of your body slips away, velvet before touch.

I discover the pale white of you. One light in the room
brands you. In fine detail, you quiver, begin a word you never finish.

Snow reaches its stillness in the crisscrossing of the maple's tree branches,
dark edges of winter on the window pane. We will not intrude.

Hair, pulled away from your face, lies in the palms of my hands.
No music, candlelight, opened doors—the quiet of the pillow

underneath your head, the moon slipping in as promised,
white sheets blanketing our private earth. My finger silences

your opening lips, language only in night's whispers...
whispers, then, in our slipping away.

Ultrasound

The time is 15:54:59.
The technician greases my tummy
and looks for signs of life.
I'm getting a probe type, line B 3.50 MH2
Section D, Mode 1B ultrasound.

The numbers, the letters, my stare...
first the wall, then, the ceiling,
finally, the sterile curtains—
white, floor to ceiling,
closed, wall to wall.

And then, the curtains open—
a medicinal shaft of light,
and I pause for a moment
between dark and light
before I become vertical.

In the gray triangle against black
background photo, you are only
seven weeks and one day old,
and already your heart beats within mine.

"Caring...is what we do best," states the caption.
I prepare to leave, your photo pressed
between my two unwashed hands,
walk down stairs one very small step at a time

until the morning sun knows no clouds
in the periwinkle blue sky, and my hand
glides across my tummy to touch
one brilliant ray of you.

For my daughter, Maggie

At the Playground

Soon, after birth, she swings back and forth,
higher and higher, her little body fixed
in the small swing, unknowing smile
on her pixie face, weightless once again
in my womb of no fear.

Now, only at her thirteenth month,
she searches for my face
at the top of her flight.
The top is higher, higher still,
the swing too small when large
tree branches still hover over her

and wind rocks her back and forth
in her new upside down world
where she is taller, wider, just enough depth
to scream when the sky takes her.

My Little Girl Wakes Up

Morning sunlight in fleeting shadow
casts its small image on the kitchen wall.
Maggie Fay swipes at the shadow,
then pulls back her tiny hand.
Sunlight, elusive, slips through
the spaces between her fingers.

The blow dryer on my adult hair
does not frighten her anymore.
She even accepts the sound
of the coffee grinder, former kitchen
monster, abusing the quiet of dawn.

If she cannot touch or own light and dark,
cannot love them like a play doll or stuffed bear,
shadow will still be her inseparable companion,
imaginary real friend and enemy.

Soon, she will sit with the girl doll, clothe it with care,
note its matching blouse and skirt, high heels and shiny bracelets.
Later she will strangle the doll with its own hair, a prelude
to decapitation, ripped clothing, broken legs, and one high heel
thrown into a pile of other solitary heels.

And she will be pleased as her two ice-blue eyes stare down dead doll eyes.
Only then can she sleep with the faded brown tattered bear between her arms
every night and treasure as a jewel each loose button
from the bear's vest stored under her bed.

She will keep close watch on doll and bear
sitting on the same shelf next to each other in the dark,
in the night, in the silence of being an only child—

then, in her twilight, the shelf angling, threatening
to break from the wall when she tosses over from sleep
into nightmare, the bear loose on the floor.

Holy Saturday

The day before Easter, my three-year old, Maggie, hands on hips,
expects the resurrection of the sun when she cries out to sidewalks
drenched with a full week's rain, *I spank you rain, I spank you!*

I see puddles and no promise of Resurrection,
    how well I listened to the absence of song
in Lent's long journey to the Cross
    where the dirge filled me with nails, wood, and screams.
How Holy this Saturday when the world recedes
    in darkness from hail, tornado, hurricane.

Still, I want to thank Maggie, applaud her wrath at water.
From here, she can take on volcanoes and earthquakes,
keep her little-girl defiance, remind me, as Lent always will,

to demand the Resurrection.

Picking up a Child

I. December

Fierce, the father's walk down the street of winter's edge
on the almost dark afternoon. He will pick up Penelope from school.
He carries the red kindergarten mittens she left on the kitchen table
in her haste, preferring love of school to warm hands.

Now, he rubs his bare hands together as if at a campfire
with six-year-old son, Ethan. Step by step the father walks
down the fragile sidewalk, avoids the monster cracks.

How many steps taken away from that day drenched in August light?
His pace toward school becomes slow,
    then as calculated as his ninety-degree turn
to avoid an ice patch. He marvels at his cunning, his automatic quick steps,

his body still standing upright. He lingers, looks at the ice,
imagines the smooth glide of a skater before her partner
picks up her feather-light body with ease.

School is in sight, safe curtained windows framing snow
and the traced children's hands that touch small flakes
as if to play with them.

II. Last August

Its stubborn refusal to enter autumn.
He stands with Ethan—deep, peaceful waters—
shore at their backs, other children on the beach
with only their feet in the water, as melted ice cream sticks to sand
like school glue to paper, their laughter moving farther away
as the diminished waves meet the caress of land.

He holds Ethan next to him, sees the gentle water
melt their sunburned arms, glass droplets clinging to their noon skin.
Subterranean tempest makes their feet snap like twigs from the lake's floor,
their bodies scooped up and tossed yards deeper.

Sunlight invades the retina, water opens tight lips,
two bodies turn away and toward each other.
Then, he feels the paper skin of childhood wrap itself around his ankles,
then his knees, followed by a grasping of his waist.

He gains firm footing just long enough to give it up,
reach for Ethan, raise his feather-light body,
shoreline canceled. Water ascends, prism of light,
his life not even a grain of sand, his son's grows large
as he swallows the imprisoned silence of his prayer.

Unknowing water envelops his son,
soundless invisible depths—prayer's answer.
They are permitted one framed moment:
fingertips meet, an opening to touch
this slippery letting go.

A liquid curtain separates them,
rising and falling, rising and falling—
No ropes. No stage lights.

He, the one-person audience,
tries to part the curtain,
his hand slashing away at the fabric,

a demi-god mutilating loss to trace
what he did not choose: the small body
mirrored into him, leaving like a birth,
like a stillness, into dark, into light. Into...

In loving memory of Ethan Seitzer

Daze in Burlington, Iowa

I.

I see you before you see me,
sitting on a train station bench—
solitary man waiting for the late train.

The conductor helps me down the platform,
with genteel man-to-woman courtesy.
So far I have not stumbled.

The train pulls out of the now trainless station,
we hug, too proper, my backpack
a clumsy barrier until embrace hijacks us.

My hair, you say, looks different.
I think gold, auburn, gray,
the fine-tuned mixture of youth, old age.

Sunday in Burlington as I watch
the train head for its next stop, Mount Pleasant,
the ghost of our not seeing each other for

twenty-five years lingers on the train platform
while you usher me into a borrowed, stumbling car
halting, igniting, halting, igniting.

II.

Then, the unplanned smile marks both our faces
at the same instant, the laughter at broken glass bottles
trying to break an already broken car.

In your shaking car, we pull into your driveway.
You walk in front of me, a confident stride. I see the man
who will wear the same green shirt Sunday to Wednesday

and owns but one fork and knife,
a man who lives in a renovated Standard Oil Station
with pictures on his wall of Ezra Pound, Hilda Dolittle,

Dorothy and the Scarecrow,
Abraham Lincoln staring out into your yet-to-be-repaired car
while Jimmy Dean beckons to us from the wall:

Rebel, ride a motorcycle, don't take no
for an answer. Fifteen guitars, three guns,
six shelves of books, all of them read.

A man who puts stray bullets near
the gas station's entrance—tells me this
scares off thieves, marauders, psychos.

A man with no reliable stock of groceries
and skulls and crossbones for decorations
on his bathroom curtains, a man who sometimes

walks naked in the dark of his huge yard,
stars sheltering him while pine trees stand
as sentinels that spite the wind.

III.

Four days of your motorcycle repairs,
my viewing the Mississippi River
from different heights, angles,

crossing bridges, long pauses over currents,
lying on a plot of green grass between two pine trees,
shedding first a book, then my shoes, then my watch,

wanting the grass to stain me,
for sunlight to sift through me,
not know where it begins and I end.

Occasional revving up startles the nothingness,
the motorcycle starts up, then falters.
Freight trains, giant loudspeakers,

luminescent right across your back yard.
Four days we live without
television, road maps, or Bibles,

but there is a religion between us.
We sleep in separate chaste beds,
but there is a religion between us.

At night when you dream of a car
that starts, a motorcycle that runs,
I dream I am Jimmy Dean chasing

Dorothy down that yellow brick road until I
become the scarecrow that comes to see a man
who lives on the side of the highway,

the traffic-filled one not taken.
Perhaps I will tell my husband I love you
with no garment shed between us,

not even a kiss on the cheek, and he will
do something rebellious like not getting mad,
or instinctual, like going back to bed.

IV.

My train going home is late,
so I am benched with you at the station.
Still, we are right on time, the two of us,

fit right in it at that moment.
I can miss the train,
I can take the train.

When I am gone and the white moon
centers itself in black Wednesday night sky,
when we shiver in the middle of the week

from our loss of beginnings and endings,
and awaken from the same dream, station-less,
think of Chicago and Burlington,

the long river separating our states,
meandering along, seeping into Iowa and Illinois,
water as offering to land.

V.

In some dreamless portion of
Wednesday/Thursday, in synchronized
no rapid eye movement,

cars, motorcycles will stumble across Mississippi bridges,
their breadth unknown in the star-less/star-filled
shimmering twilight of dawn.

They will stumble, falter,
awaken to their engines;
Pulse, ignite, tremble…

at the offering of another day.

Walking the Path toward Home

Yesterday at twilight I passed a field of lilacs.
They dwindled into shadow,
a memory of purple as the night grew large.

I did not pick the lilac
though I lingered over its scent
and imagined spring filled with unborn children.

I walked through the field to know what I did not pick.
The value of the lilac remained
as it swayed in the wind, free from my touch.

I left the field, walked slowly down the measured path
to where the sweet aroma of all that I have picked
was borne to fill my home.

At Home

Thanksgiving Day the sweet smell of pine
rises past the tallest tree, the wind conspiring:
You are nobody's daughter, mother, aunt, niece.

Out of town near the California coastline,
your past above the mountains in mist,
with each step, you are not you.

The ocean moves back from you.
You take another step toward it as the fog rolls in,
feel a chill that is yours alone, like footprints.
No mother tells you to button up; you'll catch cold.

While the seagull lifts its wings, the constants come back,
a litany of smells—turkey, cranberries, pumpkin—
and drift away into snow and long walks.

You are at home far away
with this feast of solitude
that needs no dressing.

The wild gull soars.
Sky, ducks, cold embrace of ocean wind,
blessed to call you family.

The Coffee Percolator on the Gas Stove

At camp, when I hear water boil
and the pot lid dance to celebrate
the color brown rising to the top,
I know that soon I will befriend the morning.

Other designer coffees try to replace you
in sleek stylish pots, dripping caffeine jolts
into being as early as 4:00 a.m. for internet lovers
needing a fix of information.

I stare at dawn through a plain window,
its curtain framing quiet August trees,
lake waters sleeping next to the shoreline
and only one bird singing to the morning,

tentative, not yet off the tree.
I sit, warm cup in cold hands,
drink my Folgers, a sip at a time,
I have all the information I need.

In praise of Camp Nawakwa, Lac du Flambeau, North Woods of Wisconsin

Penciled-in Places

He heard the voices after Christmas,
pronouncement of the end of angels.
January a forever thing, February
a blister on his soul never breaking,
March not even coming in with a candle's light,
only wars and soldiers in his head,
first a whisper, then a conspiracy
of winking eyes, then a shout.

April came uninvited
as he waited furiously for showers,
for the redemption of May,
thought he saw a flower one day,
some sort of red white blue illusion
that disappeared with no warning
into June, and one day he thought he saw sunlight
in his night dreams, but it was no dream at all
of night or day or hope.

Still, the earth had turned these six months,
and he felt a tilting in himself,
then entered July's slow return to darkness.

October, school in full force,
August and September only an afterthought,
a sneering report card about to arrive in November,
some sort of mid-semester warning sign
that it had been winter all along,
that December was nothing more
than the end of unnoticed years,
jungles of seconds, minutes, quartered hours
breaking out of the glass of old grandfather clocks.

And the wind blew upside down,
and the sun crashed into the unfailing stars.
The moon suddenly jumped in the sky,
began to rotate, revolve, reverse,
and dawn arose as an accident of night,
and the kitchen calendar went backward,
and nobody ate in the scheduled penciled-in places
of December, November, October.

The sun skipped over months,
as if they were pebbles,
then slew both lion and lamb.
February, a hint of whisper,
January, the silence of snow
on starlight nights in forests
of unseen animals.

Then, he stood above city traffic
five or ten flights up or down,
and gave his last salute.
Knowing his body would
turn with the unstoppable earth,
he let go of unsure feet and flew
briefly with wonder, no hesitation,
landing like a beautiful animal, seen.

For Scott Shaeffer, 25

Marking the Days

I. December

"Do Not Enter" on the room door.
Breathless, I enter through darkness,
know I have not trespassed.

Gray. Muted walls, steady fall of snow
beyond the window, quieting the earth.

I hug your stillness,
linger in the interstice
between life and death,
your memory my child.

Will your spirit fill me now?
Your body, so still, mine so trembling.
I kiss your face, touch your closed eyes
for you to see beyond.

Then, you release me to the world.
I leave you, hands gliding your hair,
a last snow flake finding its way through shadow.

II. January

Now, I mark for remembrance
the day you were born, the evening you died,
as if I could forget in wintered,
unmarked days where one is another's coming.

Time's healer of nothing.

III. February

I've not fixed my watch,
have thrown out all clocks
but the one with no second hand,
a reminder I still belong to earth.
I wait to be with you—

child of your womb again,
sitting on your lap. I speak with you
daily, walk with you through
each drift of snow. The night comes

for me too. Away from my twilight path
I too will drift and, like you,
will know the grace of snow,

how, star-guided, it glided
from God's skilled hands
blinding us, binding us.

For my Mother, in loving memory

Ode to Glacier National Park in August

The red tour bus seats 17 of us all intent to see every silver/white glacier.
We might miss something which is why there is no top to the bus,
and we can stand on cue for fresh air and sights.

Every vista is even better than we imagined it, each turn in the road
a new miracle of height, sediment, ancient ripple marks and mud cracks.
We learn that Mount Wilbur is a classic glacier horn
    carved by glaciers on all sides.

In the Siyeh Formation, gray limestone towers above us
where Stromatolite fossils appear as heads of darkened cabbage
etched into silver/white rock. They contain some of the earliest forms of life.
The Appekenny and Grinnell formations even announce rainbow impressions
in the bright green and barn red mudstones.

The driver wakens me from my trance, reminds us
we are traveling down Going to the Sun Road, but my mind turns
to the five-sided lavender columbine at the side of the road.

Soon the park will close for longer than it is open.
Its open roads will fill with 30 feet of snow as a slice
of silver moon casts soft light on the darkness beneath it.

Anonymity will cover Lakes McDonald, Bowan, and St. Mary.
Still, I will think of them and flower and tree—
and the glacier that grows smaller with each passing year,
and how the very park itself will hibernate like the bear.

The tour comes to its close, and I should be bone-tired,
but a deeper sleep will come, absent of earth and me.

Leaving Glacier National Park

I will remember the afternoon hike,
how I turned one way and not the other,
saw the white clouds embrace the rim of a mountain,
how the mountain accepted the sky.

I caught your hand and said *Look, look!*
You turned.
It is as though God is staring at us.
You did not laugh.

You captured my hand.
We stood there a moment silent as mountains
accepting the gentle rainfall on our faces
and did not move.

For my husband, Jim Szmurlo

Little Girl Boards the Train

I wait for the train to come into my very own station,
the beginning of spring flowering, the cure for my impatience.
Then, the deafening stroke of my father's hands
placed firmly on both my shoulders, announcing *no*.
Too late, train left station, put the tears back in your eyes.

But I soon learn to glisten onwards,
see past the narrow geography of daughter.
I learn waiting at stations until my time comes
and no one can stop me from traveling
down the route I knew I would take all along,

broad, aimless, laughing away directions.
I will not be the tossed-away weed, and the train
will not move on without me. *Yes,* the exquisite flower
of train meeting track at night, when no one is looking,
carries me into the glittering dawn of my journey.

Trained

I smell the Amtrak trip I took today, yesterday—
body sweat from planning, the rosemary in the pasta
eaten in the dining car in slow motion over the Mississippi River.

I am the ache of insomnia, the ambition of travel,
lead legs that cannot in coach twist or turn
into the length of sleep.

Station signs stare at me, and I know I want to
get off, go home, go away.

I miss everything I left behind:
the dog's last knowledge of me as he sits on my lap,
the cats mesmerized by their eternal absence of ambition
and fascination with hiding under blankets,
the fish I envy for their smooth glide through water
when they go nowhere…and get there.

At the station, my husband's blue-gray eyes already register loss.
We wait together; my bulging suitcases shout *no turning back now!*

My eyes have stayed open for so long that I seem to see everything:
the printout of five changes of arrival and departure times,
the unmade bed I left in Chicago,
the writers' conference I will attend near a Minnesota lake,
the zipper that will surely break on my suitcase
if I add even a Q-tip, a peanut, another writing goal.

Let me just rest in accomplishment, sleep inside let-it-be.
Train travel will bookmark the sunlight I left behind,
lead me to the lucid new landscape that will only come
from closed eyes and the bloom of unplanned dreaming.

"May I Have This Dance?"
Chicago, 1944

Suited, he eyes her from a distance across the dance floor.
Will she turn me down like all the others?
Jazz and Big Band dismiss self-doubt and past history.

His mother deserted him after the stock market crashed.
Polio thick in his legs, lost with his younger sister
in dark, paralytic adolescence in long Midwestern winters
when snow glistened on the slippery dance floor of the earth, he crawled
the last stretch back to home to deliver Catholic Charity coupons
so his family could eat, crutches stolen by town bullies.

Dressed in pearls and the clinging dress showing off her legs,
she sees him, sees he is looking at her, and she bends from her waist
to tighten a loose high heel.
Will he ask me to dance?
She never thought herself pretty, with her slightly slumped shoulders,
her crooked teeth. But now she is Ginger Rogers eying Fred Astaire.

He takes the first step, his stature certain, planned.
The walk across the dance floor is long. "May I have this dance?"
not yet spoken, lodges in his throat, threatening to choke him.

Only five words. He takes more steps, sees her smile, her wavy hair.
She sees his tall dark and handsome trump his polio limp.
The word *yes* and the first dance begins.

"Crippled," the albatross the bullies made him wear,
disappears in the swirling white lights,
velvet gold tapestry, royal-blue carpeted entrances—

no hint of any of it leaving after midnight
as he holds her in his arms, his old crutches vanishing
as he enters the fairy tale, a prince.

Benny Goodman, Glen Miller, Andy Kirk.
Clouds of Joy in each trombone, trumpet, saxophone—
bass guitar married to the drum beat, the down beat.

Then, that final ascent to gleaming chandelier heights,
Ginger's diamond necklace and ring, Fred light as feather,
beneath them the polished shine of the Aragon Ballroom floor.

He bows. *Thank you for the dance.* She curtsies.
Roses, scented letters, champagne toasts, the forever
of the Aragon Ballroom marquee giving light to their dark.

In memory of my parents, Edward and Leona Skelly,
married February 10, 1945

Ode to Montana

Praise to the flat lands of Montana,
green, brown, telephone pole background.

To the stretching acres viewed through train windows,
dead cars, pickup trucks, just one driver at the train stop.

Praise to this spacious state with an occasional silver silo,
one green tree in an otherwise empty landscape.

For the Bud Light truck driver with the road to himself,
the few cows grazing next to the train.

Praise to bales of hay, small wooden houses,
the odd quiet of a stationary tractor.

To Montana, where time passes slowly,
in the ripe August presence of now.

Night Train East of Denver

Lightning leaves the Rockies, ignites new sky,
its insomniac bolts strike silver pillow clouds,
free fireworks for restless travelers.

The mile-high city recedes into black ink sky,
train begins its slow descent, not yet wanting
the pull of gravity to prairie flatlands.

How striking our cocooned safety!
This lullaby of wheels delivers
each inch of track for us to savor.

Telephone wires and the industrial night roll past us,
a reel from an old silent movie. The train's engineer
plays the horn, a soft light glowing inside our veins.

Each passing house, each lonely car driver on deserted roads,
a target for flickering celestial devils who know not why
they strike a match at sleeping stars as we crawl in peace to lower land.

Passenger

It is time for the bright day of the soul.

I.

The morning train brings good reading,
train stops announced, not ignored.
Detraining, I see my friends before they see me,
scanning the crowd to pick me out, like a flower.

Sunlight sifts through lake water,
swimming our Holy Communion,
children play with beach toys.

The woman in the French deli offers us free wine,
an old world charm in her handling of bottles
that filter delicious rays of noon sunlight
before their pouring into crystal stemmed glasses.

The smiles of strangers belong to us.
The cards we see in the French deli are hand made,
beautiful to frame, not send.

Scented massage oil lingers on my hand,
the sales lady's satin, smooth-textured voice,
her smile when we buy, when we only look.

At dinner, one large tree in the back yard—
all that is needed for canopy.
Our small table, green candle,
day gradually fading into night.

We know the garden green peppers and tomatoes
are not quite ripe,
that the settling of dusk is a blanket
covering infant grass.

II.

The car ride to my train quiets our incessant talk—
religion, God, the afterlife.
The best answers to all our questions live inside the home
of many unlocked doors, many wide-open windows.

Then, beer drinkers a third my age fill the train,
laugh at the wonder of turning 21,
scream about free beer birthdays,
do not know which stop to get off or even the train's direction.

I sit in the quiet on a newspaper-free seat,
reading *The Cloud of Unknowing* by an unknown fourteenth century author,
a book so thick with prescription on how to know God
that I welcome my book marker, look up at youth, remember mine.

The conductor snaps pictures of beer cans, faces full of tomorrow.
I hear absence of annoyance in my voice and his
when we offer congratulations to strangers.

Towns slip away,
their always unveiled homes hear the train's whistle
as we move out of the station.

I know no one will meet me as I detrain,
know that I will move into midnight alone,
lose my direction, yearn for its return,
cross over tracks and look both ways.

Street lamp lights bending over sidewalks bless the night,
summer wind sifts through trees, cools my face.

It is the right time.

For Stan and Mary Perrin

Taizé Prayer

The movement toward absolute silence
in waning candlelit darkness,
"so hard to achieve," I can feel us all thinking.

The cell phone rings sharply, madly, with its own life force.
The driven car passes by our stained glass window,
my stomach growls while I dictate it to stop.

We want the silence more than blood,
single-minded congregation motionless,
in waiting, until it catches us all by surprise.

If only for a few moments…
time, thought, speech, breath
disappear.

Lost in evening, this Communion is Holy,
this Darkness complete, and we are halted.
Disciples first looking…then seeing.

In appreciation of Saint Gertrude Church, Chicago, Illinois

Winter Birds

Freezing weather, snow angling,
and still the birds chirp—
January too early for their winter.

We walk through dark streets with childlike purpose,
though street lamps cast shadows in our paths,
fold our hands together,

winter upon winter,
trying once again to keep
the bite of frost at bay.

If we see better
than dimly through a blizzard,
will we bother to look at all?

If, even at winter's end,
the silence of what we still do not know
slaps us in the face like an angry parent,

we should be as we always were:
children fluttering before a faltering fire,
gathering our strength as we would before birth,

the dream of keeping out cold on our breath
just a lift of the wing away.

Lucent

I have slipped away from
the harsh parameters
of the defined body—
arms, legs, now electric.
I have left her
supine in noon sun,
the willow lucent and green,
its canopy shelters
the brown river that lightens
the moment I step into it
for the second time.

Without a Leash

Falling as effortlessly as leaves into our dreams,
no siren or clock awakens us.

Paws, arms mingle,
my heart feels his beat, his legs extend
into a separate world from mine.

Our eyes have closed together, weary travelers we,
two bodies meld in our respite from fatigue.

In the still of our leash-less dreams, we run far away,
for running is all that matters.

I run far away from myself, a sprint born
from my two magic feet catapulting me
into the nether-land between my life and his death.

And I tremble.

He into his eternal watch over me,
a four-footed God gliding over calm waters,
the embrace of his fur against my skin

Silencing.

For my dog, Marky

Falling

in love, through a trap door.

I cannot step in or into time,
nor can I reach the floor.

I don't go down on bended knee,
plea for the other to catch me.

It would be cliché to remark
on the loss of self or the need
for salve, for darkness.

For falling in love
only leaves the old self still standing
secured in sunlight, the severity of vision.

Social silence still stands. I talk to no one.
Secrets stutter on lips that almost move.

One high tidal wave took me
for a ride, for a shoreline.

Neither mist nor madness matter
on a night too thick with my own presence on a deserted beach,
when before I was taken I dropped the letter on the sand,
saw my words whimper in the absence of all light,
saw the calm and quiet of deep sea before the tempest,
before I shook off all clothing,
had nothing to call my own but my closed eyes.

Why Do They Shut Me Out of Heaven?

Did I sing too softly, a perched bird
looking down at earth as if it would be
the only place that would have me?

I am not flower or song or even one
of thousands of buds in June.

Why do they shut me out of heaven?

Did I sit too long on the same cushioned chair
looking out of my life-long window at rain and dark—
sounds of cloud bursts and dripping muted
by panes and all openings locked?

Later, snow alighting on the pane, feather light,
God's first winter whisper as my warm coffee
sits still in the cup on the ledge. Should I drink it?

Why do they shut me out of heaven?

Should I shelve my view from the window?
No, the flight of several birds now shocks me.
The uniformity of their ascension pulls at my assigned heart
and the measured leafless window sill that knows
not even one egg from one nest.

How strapping this chair I sit on!
And now I can only whisper:
Why do they shut me out of heaven?

My cat beckons for touch,
the servant closes the curtains,
brings me more coffee, newspaper at the ready,
kindling in the fireplace, kindly turning into flame,
the error of my life going up in smoke, then the inevitable smoldering,
a nest of demons for my eyes only, dancing among the ashes,
a mockery of the only quotidian life I chose.

After Emily Dickinson

Sonnet in Praise of "Lux Aeterna"*

Quiet these violin strings in their first search for light.
Then, a small humming, a prayer beginning to sing,
Poco ritard, but soon building to the flight
of angel voices that all around us ring.

As if we could listen and not weep...
as if we could not be filled with the mercy of dream.
Tender sopranos taking us to measures we can keep,
to deep requiem, the heaven of God's scheme.

For treasured mortals, the brilliant fate
of God's seed planted in us, sprouting as love.
From this world, we pass but once through your gate
and leave all behind us in eternal above.

God's angelic chorus within our new sight
as the curtain closes on earth's last night.

* Performed by North Shore Choral Society as part of the "Ethereal Light" Concert featuring David H. Edelfelt, Guest Conductor; Michelle Areyzaga, Soprano; and Robert Orth, Baritone, May 31, 2009, The Parish Church of Saint Luke, Evanston, Illinois. Composed by Morten Lauridsen for the Los Angeles Master Chorale and Conductor Paul Salamunovich, who gave the World Premiere in the Dorothy Chandler Pavilion on April 13, 1997.

Encomium for a Sestina

I looked hard for you today in the "all new" fourth edition of *The American*
Heritage Dictionary, a twenty-first century reference with over seventy
thousand entries and one thousand new words and meanings.

I held my breath between "sestet" and "set," but you were not to be found.
I checked again, knowing the frailty of the middle-aged eye,
but you were gone to a quiet place where the wordless live.

Sestet and sonnet both made the grade,
but what oversight or intention led you to an early grave?

Where have you gone with your six verses, each with six lines?
Your closing triplet? Your lovely two-syllable end words?
Water, city, sorrow, season, lovers, passage—
words that know each other so well, they welcome, not fear,
their constant exchange of places, as if to say to each other,
I know this spot well, and you should too!

You were complex but ego-less, no first or last words.
All six words in the triplet linger in the reader's mind:

> There is no passage to the jeweled city,
> No right of way for lovers shedding sorrow,
> I am always out of season, without water.

Now, with the passage of time, the light of your jewels dims
in the twilight celestial city, and while I don't mind my free verse,
I loved the cost of choosing six, and only six, words, your season,
its watering of my mind, the garden of my sorrow now,
for having lost you, if only for a moment, in the "all new" dictionary.

North Woods Night Sky in Autumn

Two trees tower over blades of grass,
their slight bend toward each other creates
an altar between earth and heaven.

Cloud-filled night, milky film over telescopic lenses,
the astronomer gropes in the paralyzed silence of dark
thickened by absence of wind.

Jupiter floats in and out of cloud, a white dollar coin.
For a moment, the astronomer looks up from his attempts,
witnesses the slightest shiver of wind alighting
on the leaves of both trees. The night beyond trees
takes on a different hue: slippery silver trembling moon
disappears into a permanent black ink of unknowing.

Jupiter looks down on the long expanse of continued dark,
drifts in and out of clouds, looks for its own four moons,
becomes transparent in its desire to remain unseen.

A minute passes.

The astronomer rejects the telescope, moves between the two trees,
observes the silence of their floating leaves drifting mid-air
between tree and ground, the edge of science left behind
on even the strongest lenses. A great calm comes over stars
as Jupiter moves on. The astronomer stands still
in a night with no animal sound.

Opaque night.
Translucence, though, through nodding leaves.
The earth continues its inevitable rotation
away from seeing much beyond its small self.
Clear glass on one side of the mirror between heaven and earth,
perhaps our reflection in that mirror.

Sometimes when the silence is sharper than a new knife,
when the ocean is the medium between us and the heavens,
and the astronomer looks long and hard, willing the earth
to stand still, if just for a moment,
then gaze becomes telescopic, reveals
an opening of the night's eye—stilling us, filling us.

A Distant God

I notice it most here in the North Woods:
the uncountable spaces between separate leaves and branches
where the wind takes charge of the accommodating tree—

In campfire where the same wind
sometimes hides its force,
allowing the breath of flame—

In the mesh of white and silver cloud
reflected in a pre-dawn lake
where the silence of night encounters light—
both cloud and lake obliterated
to permit their interweaving.

How distant even the earth beneath my feet feels
as I yearn for God. At times, I have carried torches
to burn the limits of my vision, to light my way into you
or perhaps ignite a new clarity of the eye.

Silenced, without station, standing as alone as the pine tree
in that one moment before the sun strips away
the union of sky and lake and clarifies their solitude as mine,
I see that I have always preferred dark, annihilation,
an earth sketched into heaven.

Now, unannounced, a team of eagles flies over my head
and crosses the lake before I notice the full shock of their wings—
how they spread to capture my sunrise.

Writing on April 24, 2013

The urge to write strikes me right now—
odd, I think, as I try not to think at all.
Why now, alone in my winter coat

in a dark car waiting to go into Target,
not knowing that a woman I love died this morning
while I was sound asleep in my own bed?

I came here to shop, but shopping is like writing:
I look a lot, buy a little, think too much,
but purchase only a few words.

Writing is not knowing where the blessing of the next word
will take me, stilling me into caring about the unknown—
the skin underneath my band-aid hiding today's biopsy,

the rain that may fall tonight, the perhaps of the red rose's first bloom.
Today's weather is too cold for April, and shopping never warms me
as I crave the purchase of words more than fine-fitting clothes.

So here I remain in the car, knowing the muse
may come…or not, but either way this poem owns me,
demands the long birth of seed into flower.

For all I know of rain and flower and what lies beneath my wounds,
I know more of my thin purchase of life—that if I buy it at all,
it will unveil me…even in the dark, even in the shadows of my own words.

For Ann O'Connor

Winter Solstice

Earth silences itself into the dark.
Leafless trees extend into longest night,
their gnarled branches arthritic fingers folded into prayer.

Earth is old, poised in the present,
desires no future, no past.

Troubled greenery departs as Earth
peeks into its own still lucid oceans,
waits, like a lover,
for the flame of the not-yet-lit candle,
appears to drift to the interstellar space traveler,
tries to see itself in its own abyss,
but has no ego or mirrors.

Starlings fly in mass
in the naked spaces between startled tree branches.

Time passes, then dies, lost to thickening darkness,
but still the quiet drift out of gravity, pulled by angels
to some birth our eyes will never see.

Publishing Credits

Stories

Bus Fare. Short Story Nominated for Illinois Arts Council Award. *Black Maria Magazine*. Vol. 4, No. 1, 1980. Chicago, IL. Revised since its original publication.

Looking for Home. *Primavera Magazine*. Vol. 6-7, 1981. University of Chicago, Chicago, IL. Revised since its original publication.

Listening to Mozart. *The Village Rambler*. Chapel Hill, NC, 2005. Revised since its original publication.

Poems

Some of the published poems in this book have been revised since their original appearance.

Flight after Marathon. *Embers and Flames*. Edited by Whitney Scott, Outrider Press, Dyer, IN, June 2015.

Paps Sings the Blues, My Father Waits for Me (formerly My Father is Waiting for Me), The Same Night (formerly For Steve), Strangers and Friends, At the Playground (formerly My Daughter Grows Afraid of Swings), Holy Saturday (formerly Taking on Tornadoes), Walking the Path toward Home, Winter Birds. *Before We Reach the Sky*, Chicago, IL, 1993.

At the Playground (formerly My Daughter Grows Afraid of Swings) was awarded a second place prize, and Winter Birds was awarded a first place prize in the Poets and Patrons Contest, Evanston, IL, 1990. After its first publication in *Before We Reach the Sky*, it was published in its original form in the online book titled *Book of Inspirations*, Dominican Shrine of Saint Jude Thaddeus. Chicago, IL, 2009. Revised and republished in *A Bird in the Hand*. Edited by Whitney Scott, Outrider Press, Dyer, IN, 2011.

Etiquette for Former Chicago Lovers (formerly The Girl He Left Behind), *Daily Differences Anthology*, Chicago, IL, 1987.

Past the Stars. *Rambunctious Review*. Vol. VI, Number 1, Chicago, IL, 1989.

Anatomy of a Woman. *Thirty Days*. The Best of the Tupelo Press 30/30 Project's First Year. Edited by Marie Gauthier, Tupelo Press, North Adams, MA, 2015.

Whisper (formerly New Moon). *Falling in Love Again*. Edited by Whitney Scott, Outrider Press, Crete, IL, 2005. New Moon was awarded a third place prize as part of its publication in this anthology.

Ultrasound (formerly Ultrasound, July 19, 1988). *Korone*, Vol. 6., Womanspace Center, Rockford, IL, 1990.

Leaving Glacier National Park. *The Mountain*. Edited by Whitney Scott, Outrider Press, Dyer, IN, 2014.

Daze in Burlington, Iowa. *Off Channel*. Midwest Writing Center. Davenport, IA, 2012.

At Home. *Heart*. Vol. 3. Orangeburg, SC, 2008.

The Coffee Percolator on the Gas Stove. Originally published in *Vacations: The Good, the Bad, and the Ugly*. Edited by Whitney Scott, Outrider Press, Dyer, IN, 2006. Revised and republished in *Cram 10*. Edited by C.J. Laity, Chicago, IL, 2010.

Penciled-in-Places, First Place Award, Free Verse Category Division. Poets and Patrons. Downers Grove, IL, October, 2012. Finalist status for the Gwendolyn Brooks Poetry Contest through the Guild at the Chopin Theater, Chicago, IL, June 2011.

Taizé Prayer, Second Place Award, Adult Category Division, Niles Public Library, Niles, IL, May 2009, and published in *Book of Inspirations*. Dominican Shrine of Saint Jude Thaddeus, Chicago, IL, 2009.

Encomium for a Sestina, First Place, Adult Category Division. The Thirty-first Annual Jo-Anne Hirshfield Memorial Poetry Awards. Evanston Public Library, Evanston, IL, April 2009.

Acknowledgments

This first book of mine did not come easy, by any means. Still, much of the time, I felt it was worth the effort, and I am glad that Greg Pierce, Publisher of ACTA Publications, saw something in my poetry that he seemed to like instantly. I will never forget how quickly he got back to me once he read roughly 10-15 poems. It was something like two days. Even my best writer friends, family, and certainly other publishers would never get back to me with what I considered to be electrifying speed. I am also grateful for the time and energy that Mike Coyne of In Extenso Press and Patricia Lynch of Harvest Graphics spent on this book as well—Mike proofreading and editing and Patricia doing graphics and typesetting.

Several fiction writers and poets were instrumental for me, providing editing, conversation, and new ways to look at the revision process. The short story "Standing in the Dark with my Family" went through so many revisions that by the time it went to print, I felt that I and been standing and running through the dark for years. Fiction writer Sheri Joseph pointed out some flaws in the logic of the story and urged me to go into greater and more specific detail at times. Catherine Fitzpatrick, novelist, made me see what kind of response a careful reader like herself might have. It is easy to think that every word does not count as much in short story writing as it does in poetry writing. Because of her, I learned to use the same critical eye on "Standing in the Dark with my Family" that I would revising poetry. Judith Valente, a poet with other major writing talents, really thought that my poetry would get published and took the time to read many of my poems. Dennis Held, another excellent poet, read my poetry with scrutiny and forced me to pay attention to difficult things I might very well have chosen to ignore. From him and other writers, I started to learn to not force the writing so much. Not easy for a woman as wedded to ambition as much as I am. Poet Kim Addonizio made me realize that just because a poem won first place in a reputable contest does not mean that it is "done." Actually, I don't even know what the word "done" looks like anymore. Kate Hutchinson, where would

I be without knowing that you are out there persevering, just like me, every chance you have to get even one poem written? Our friendship since graduate school has led to both of us getting closer and closer (and sometimes arriving) at becoming the best possible writers we can be. And my sister Carol Gloor, a very gifted poet, makes me laugh with her wonderful wit and justified sarcasm about writing and getting published. I am a writer less alone in the world because of her love and compassion.

I am also quite grateful for the Poetry Pilgrimage Group at St. Gertrude Church of Chicago—in particular, Mary Grover, the facilitator of the group, and regular attendees Roy Lipscomb, Regina May, and Rose Marie Anichini —all of whom provided amazing insights into the poem "Marking the Days." Please forgive me if I forgot to mention anybody else in this group who support- ed me with the revision of this poem.

I thank Steve Leek as well, another poet, who pointed out my need to over-explain my poems, along with his valiant efforts at, as he worded it so adeptly, taking the "schmaltz" out of my poems. And he is right in that I can be as stubborn as a mule at times, albeit a nice mule!

I also thank essayist Joseph Epstein for taking the time to read my poetry even though essay writing seems to be his forte. Anyone who bemoans the loss of poetry books lining our shelves is someone worth knowing. Also, reading his essays gave me a bit of faith that I could write them well if I put my mind to it.

I appreciate as well Camille Stagg as well for her wisdom and savvy pertain- ing to the publication world.

Without the Edgewater Singers of Chicago and the North Shore Choral Society of Evanston, I never would have had the incentive, to say nothing of the joy, of writing the essay "Lovely Invasion of Soul." To all the singers I have known and sung with, I thank you as well for taking me out of the sometimes too inward-oriented experience of writing poetry.

There are friends and family who have meant a lot me as I travel down this difficult and lonely road. Years ago Linda Hogan saw that my strength and a good sense of my identity were present in my poems. And Joy Bertone, my good friend since second grade, has made me laugh about my writing trials and does not run away from my tears. Greer Gilmore? Now there is a woman who appreciates both my singing and writing adventures. JoAnn Van Gilder has remained steadfast in her love and appreciation of my poetry, and Nancy Bujnowski has offered such sincere praise and offers great support in the way of organizing a poetry book party.

For all those who shall remain nameless, I thank you for sharing some of the most intimate moments of your lives with me. I treasure your vulnerability, honesty, and your trust in me as a writer. Bless all of those folks who told me to stick with it and all of those folks who told me to take a break. I listened well to both of you.

I am thankful as well for one particular place that will always live deeply in my soul—Camp Nawakwa in the Northern Woods of Wisconsin. I am a better and more peaceful person for having been there, and the way this setting inspires me to write poetry takes my breath away. And where would I be without Chicago, the setting of much of what is in this book.

No words are praiseworthy enough for my husband, Jim, who deserves a medal for listening to me scream at the computer. I will always love you and be grateful for the many ways you have made writing possible for me. And I thank my daughter Maggie for simply being who she is now, and for who she was as a small child inspiring some of the best writing in this book. And, as always, the memory of my parents is with me every day and lives as a treasure in some of these poems.

Last, but not least, all praise and glory go to the Chorus of Unpublished Poets. I could not have written this book without being one and without knowing so many of you. As for the sub-title of this book, *On Not Giving Up on Your Dream*, for once I will part with those words knowing that I did not.

About the Author

Marjorie Skelly has won first-place in the Poets and Patrons and the Jo-Anne Hirshfield Poetry Memorial awards contests, along with reaching finalist status for the Gwendolyn Brooks Poetry Slam in Chicago and twice reaching semi-finalist status with the Word Works Washington Prize. Various incarnations of her short story "Standing in the Dark with my Family," which appears in print for the first time in this book, were three times given finalist status with the prestigious *Glimmer Train Journal*, and her short story "Pass the Candied Yams," not in this collection, won second place in a National Organization for Women contest. "Bus Fare," also appearing in this book, was nominated for an Illinois Arts Council award. Skelly has taught English at Loyola University of Chicago and Northeastern Illinois University and poetry and fiction writing at a variety of venues.